MARYLAND TRIVIA

The Center for the Study of Human Systems

PO Box 235, Front Royal, VA 22630

Founded by Dr. Gilbert in 1998, the Center's mission is to make the knowledge and benefits of Bowen family systems theory as widely available as possible. The Center disseminates information and organizes seminars and leadership training programs for parents, clergy, and organizational leaders.

Extraordinary Leadership Seminars are based on Bowen theory, which leads to improved individual functioning and leadership effectiveness in the important relationship systems of life.

Seminars meet one full day a month (October through June) over a three-year cycle. They are conducted by Dr. Gilbert and other experienced faculty members. For more information, visit our web site www.hsystems.org

THANKS. . .

. . .to Elaine Dunaway whose positive feedback inspired the frenzy of work that led to bringing this book into fruition,

. . .to Frank Giove, Mrs. Leroy Bowen, Joanne Bowen and Judy Bowen, whose reading, comments and appreciation now and over the years, gave energy and made this a better effort,

. . .to all those involved in the clergy seminars – participants, faculty and facilitators in Falls Church, Pensacola, Harrisonburg and many other places – where presentations and discussions of Bowen theory helped me to get clearer, especially Lucy Marsden Hottle, Carl Dickerson, Nicholas Lubelfeld, Scotty Hargrove, Kathleen Cauley, Bonnie Sobel, Jerry Foust, Tom Hay, Jacques Hadler, and Peggy Treadwell,

. . .to my original coach, Don Shoulberg,

. . .to the Bowen Center for the Study of the Family for being there through all the years of study and coaching when I was and still am trying to understand theory better, especially Kathleen Kerr and Roberta Holt, my coaches, and also, Michael Kerr, Dan Papero, Louise Russo, Priscilla Friesen, Victoria Harrison, Andrea Maloney Schara, Douglas Murphy, Kathleen Wiseman, Anne McKnight, Bea Flynn, Ted Beal, Mignonette Keller, Keo Miller, Marjorie Hottel, Regina Carrick, Patricia Comella, and Ruth Sagar, from each of whose thinking I have benefited,

. . .to Vail Mueller for her cover design with awe for her tremendous talent and to Jesse Mueller for keeping our computers working,

. . .to Elizabeth Foss and Kathleen Monge for their energetic assistance in research,

. . .and most especially to Joe Douglass, my loving husband, whose patient, untiring, enthusiastic and interested attitude and efforts towards computer glitches, editing, camera readying, finding and working with printers and logistics, as well as in understanding the theory, have been inspiring of themselves.

MARYLAND TRIVIA

COMPILED BY
ALBERT AND SHIRLEY MENENDEZ

Rutledge Hill Press
Nashville, Tennessee

Published by Rutledge Hill Press, Inc., 211 Seventh Avenue North, Nashville, Tennessee 37219. Distributed in Canada by H.B. Fenn and Co., Ltd., 1090 Lorimar Dr., Mississauga, Ontario L5S IR7.

Typography by D&T/Bailey Typography, Nashville, Tennessee

Library of Congress Cataloging-in-Publication Data

Menendez, Albert J.
Maryland trivia / compiled by Albert and Shirley Menendez.
p. cm.
ISBN 1-55853-164-5
1. Maryland — Miscellanea. 2. Questions and answers.
I. Menendez, Shirley, 1937 – II. Title.
F181.5.M46 1992
975.2'0076 — dc20 92-6746
CIP

Printed in the United States of America
4 5 6 7 8 — 99 98 97 96

PREFACE

Maryland, though a small state, is truly America in microcosm. Its history is varied and fascinating. Its people have experienced every major event in our country's history, since it is one of the oldest states and one of the original colonies.

Moreover, its geography is diverse, encompassing mountains and seashore, the unique beauty of the Chesapeake Bay, small towns, bustling suburbs, and a world-class city. It is a state of unique and compelling personalities, from Edgar Allan Poe to Mother Seton, from Harriet Tubman to Babe Ruth. It is a state unlike any other—from its unusual state sport to its renowned cuisine.

Maryland is a civilized state in the truest meaning of that term, a state of moderation in all things, a relaxed temperament that avoids (generally) extremes in climate, behavior, or politics.

It is our fondest hope that readers of this book will want to explore further the state's history and literature, visit many of the sites described, and read some of the books mentioned.

The state is dotted with historic homes and churches and locales of scenic beauty. The official state slogan says it all, Maryland is "More Than You Can Imagine." We hope that both newcomers and natives alike will enjoy this book and find it entertaining, informative, and challenging.

Albert and Shirley Menendez
Gaithersburg, Maryland

Q. What Baltimore university, noted for its graduate schools and its renowned medical school, celebrates its centennial in 1993?

A. Johns Hopkins.

Q. Where is the state capital located?

A. Annapolis.

Q. Where did Francis Scott Key write our national anthem?

A. Fort McHenry.

Q. On what river is Annapolis situated?

A. Severn.

Q. Which small town in Frederick County is sometimes called Maryland's antique capital?

A. New Market.

Q. By what name are the counties east of the Chesapeake Bay known?

A. Eastern Shore.

Q. The Mason-Dixon Line separates Maryland from what state?

A. Pennsylvania.

Q. What is the name of the presidential retreat in the Catoctin Mountains?

A. Camp David.

Q. What westernmost county is called "America's Switzerland"?

A. Garrett.

Q. Upper Marlboro is the county seat of what county?

A. Prince George.

Q. What town served as Maryland's first capital?

A. St. Mary's City.

Q. What is the name of the prestigious liberal arts college in Frederick?

A. Hood College.

Q. Maryland shares what peninsula with Virginia and Delaware?

A. Delmarva.

Q. Where is St. Elizabeth Seton, the first U.S.-born citizen canonized by the Vatican, buried?

A. Emmitsburg.

Q. Which Maryland town has been called "The Marriage Capital of the East"?

A. Elkton.

Q. What is the county seat of Baltimore County?

A. Towson.

Q. What was the former name of the Baltimore Washington International Airport?

A. Friendship Airport.

Q. Maryland shares the Assateague Island National Seashore with which other state?

A. Virginia.

Q. What state park contains the only monument in the world dedicated to war correspondents?

A. Gathland State Park.

Q. What is Baltimore's revitalized waterfront called?

A. Inner Harbor.

Q. Which town in Allegany County was settled by Irish immigrants?

A. Mount Savage.

Q. From which part of England did many of the settlers of Smith Island come?

A. Cornwall.

—✦—

Q. Which county name means "beautiful stream" in the original Indian language?

A. Allegany.

—✦—

Q. What is the largest city on the Eastern Shore?

A. Salisbury.

—✦—

Q. Which town in Prince George's County was established by Rexford Tugwell as a New Deal experiment in "planned community" living?

A. Greenbelt.

—✦—

Q. St. Paul's Church, between Chestertown and Rock Hill, is the oldest continuously used church of what faith?

A. Episcopal.

—✦—

Q. What former chief justice of the U.S. lived at 123 South Bentz Street in Frederick?

A. Roger Brooke Taney.

—✦—

Q. What is the smallest county in the state in area?

A. Kent.

Q. Which federal government agency, of importance to senior citizens, has its main offices in Baltimore County?

A. Social Security Administration.

Q. Which Eastern Shore county is landlocked?

A. Caroline.

Q. Which nationally known Catholic charity is headquartered in Baltimore?

A. Catholic Relief Services.

Q. What is the location of the infamous facility for Confederate prisoners of war?

A. Point Lookout.

Q. Which Frederick County bridge, built in 1808, collapsed in 1942?

A. Jug Bridge over the Monocacy River.

Q. How long is the Mason-Dixon Line?

A. About 300 miles, of which 230 border Maryland.

Q. Steel mills are found in which section of Baltimore?

A. Sparrows Point.

Q. Marylanders of what ancestry are strongly represented in southeastern Baltimore?

A. Polish.

✦

Q. At what elegant hotel near Oakland did President Grover Cleveland and his bride spend their honeymoon in 1886?

A. Deer Park Hotel.

✦

Q. Roman Catholic Cardinal Edward Francis Mooney was born in which small Allegany County town?

A. Mount Savage.

✦

Q. What is the name of the early Catholic shrine located in Cecil County?

A. Old Bohemia Mission.

✦

Q. Where is the Dorchester county seat located?

A. Cambridge.

✦

Q. Which Maryland city has a "Little Italy" neighborhood known for its fine restaurants?

A. Baltimore.

✦

Q. What world-renowned Methodist missionary's ashes repose at Baltimore's Mount Olivet Cemetery?

A. E. Stanley Jones.

Q. Where did Lincoln assassin John Wilkes Booth visit a tavern on his escape route?

A. Surrattsville (now Clinton).

Q. Which Prince George's County town did the Levitt Company establish in 1960?

A. Bowie.

Q. What religious group maintains a temple in Kensington?

A. Church of Jesus Christ of the Latter Day Saints (Mormons).

Q. There was a historically large Lithuanian community in which Baltimore area?

A. Union Square.

Q. What caverns are near Boonsboro?

A. Crystal Grottoes.

Q. The Fallen Firefighters Memorial is in what town near the Pennsylvania border?

A. Emmitsburg.

Q. Which four states border Maryland?

A. Pennsylvania, Delaware, West Virginia, and Virginia.

Q. In which town can one find the Robert Morris Inn, formerly the home of the father of the financier of the Revolution?

A. Oxford.

Q. Where is the Hammond Harwood House?

A. Annapolis.

Q. In what Episcopal church on the circle in Annapolis is Sir Robert Eden, the last colonial governor, buried?

A. St. Anne's.

Q. Rockville is the county seat of which county?

A. Montgomery.

Q. Which Catholic church in Baltimore is a center of Polish customs and traditions?

A. St. Stanislaus Kostka.

Q. In which Baltimore cemetery is Francis Asbury, the "Father of American Methodism," buried?

A. Mount Olivet.

Q. Which town bordering Washington, D.C., was at one time primarily Seventh-Day Adventist?

A. Takoma Park.

Q. In which county in southern Maryland do five hundred Old Order Amish live?

A. St. Mary's.

Q. What is the name of the Annapolis college, founded in 1696, that specializes in classical studies?

A. St. John's.

Q. What was the last county established?

A. Garrett, in 1872.

Q. Who owned the elegant Baltimore mansion called Evergreen?

A. John and Alice Garrett.

Q. Where is the main campus of the University of Maryland?

A. College Park.

Q. Where is the U.S. Naval Academy?

A. Annapolis.

Q. In what town is Francis Scott Key buried?

A. Frederick.

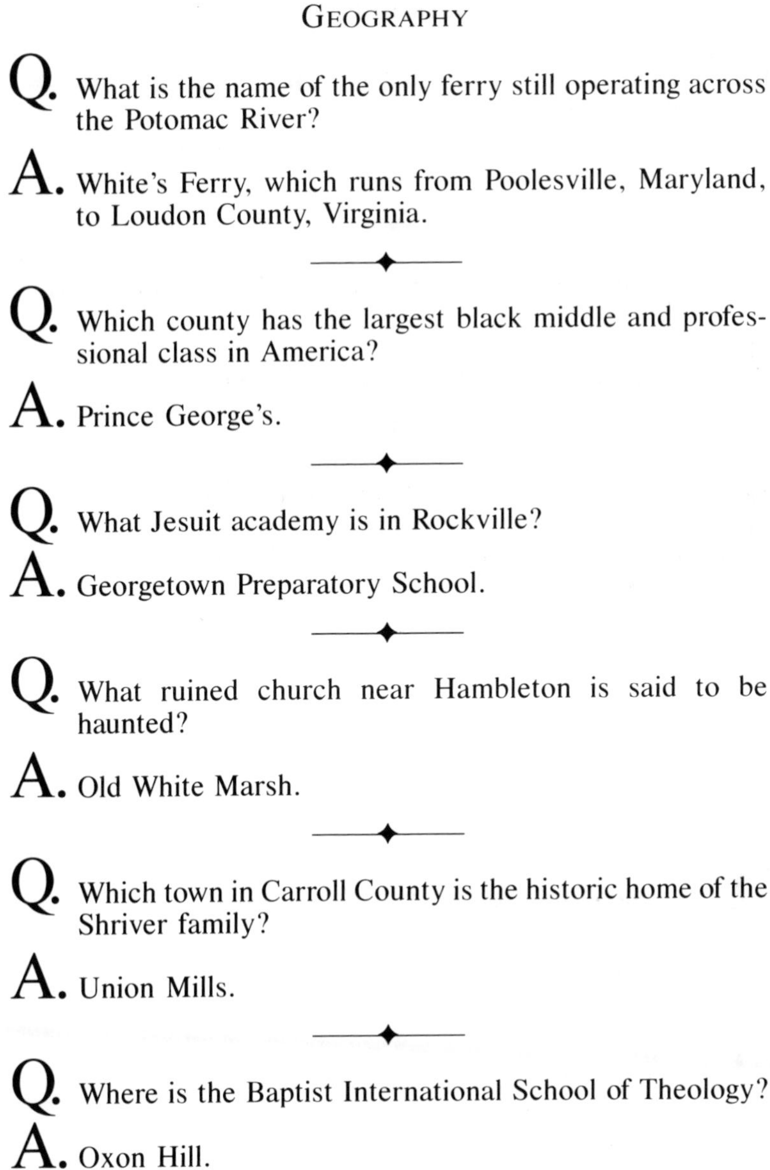

Q. What is the name of the only ferry still operating across the Potomac River?

A. White's Ferry, which runs from Poolesville, Maryland, to Loudon County, Virginia.

Q. Which county has the largest black middle and professional class in America?

A. Prince George's.

Q. What Jesuit academy is in Rockville?

A. Georgetown Preparatory School.

Q. What ruined church near Hambleton is said to be haunted?

A. Old White Marsh.

Q. Which town in Carroll County is the historic home of the Shriver family?

A. Union Mills.

Q. Where is the Baptist International School of Theology?

A. Oxon Hill.

Q. Which city calls itself the "Friendliest Town on the Eastern Shore"?

A. Pocomoke City.

Q. In which Dorchester County town were there serious racial clashes in 1963 and 1967?

A. Cambridge.

Q. What are Charles, Calvert, and St. Mary's counties often called?

A. Southern Shore or Southern Maryland.

Q. In which county is Maryland's geographic center?

A. Prince George's, four and one-half miles northwest of Davidsonville.

Q. Near what town is there a replica of the Grotto of Lourdes?

A. Emmitsburg.

Q. In what county is Fort Detrick?

A. Frederick.

Q. La Plata is the county seat of which county?

A. Charles.

Q. Which county is often called Maryland's "Last Frontier"?

A. Garrett.

Q. Which church in Oakland is called the "Church of the Presidents"?

A. St. Matthew's Episcopal, which was attended by Grant, Garfield, Harrison, and Cleveland.

Q. What is the state's largest freshwater lake?

A. Deep Creek Lake in Garrett County.

Q. What Maryland road was the first federally funded highway in the United States?

A. The National Road.

Q. Where was the first successful coke-fueled furnace in the United States?

A. Lonaconing Iron Furnace in Allegany County, which began in 1839.

Q. U.S. 40A west of Cumberland is often called what?

A. The Narrows.

Q. In what county is the Hampton National Historic Site?

A. Baltimore.

Q. In what county is Fort George Mead?

A. Anne Arundel.

Q. What is the old seaport area of Baltimore called?

A. Fells Point.

Q. Where in Baltimore is there an architectural monument honoring George Washington?

A. Mount Vernon Place.

Q. Where is Mary Surratt's house?

A. Clinton.

Q. In what Prince George's County town are tobacco auctions still held?

A. Upper Marlboro.

Q. Deal Island belongs to what county?

A. Somerset.

Q. Prince Frederick is the county seat of which county?

A. Calvert.

Q. Where was America's first Roman Catholic convent established in 1790?

A. Mount Carmel Monastery at Chandler's Hope in Charles County.

Q. Tilghman Island belongs to what county?

A. Talbot.

Q. One of America's oldest colleges, Washington College, is in which town?

A. Chestertown.

Q. What small county is said to have an unusual number of millionaires?

A. Talbot.

Q. What is the county seat of Worcester County?

A. Snow Hill.

Q. On what river did James Michener set most of his novel *Chesapeake*?

A. Choptank.

Q. Which county is sometimes called "Maryland's Best Kept Secret"?

A. Garrett.

Q. Smith Island is in which county?

A. Somerset.

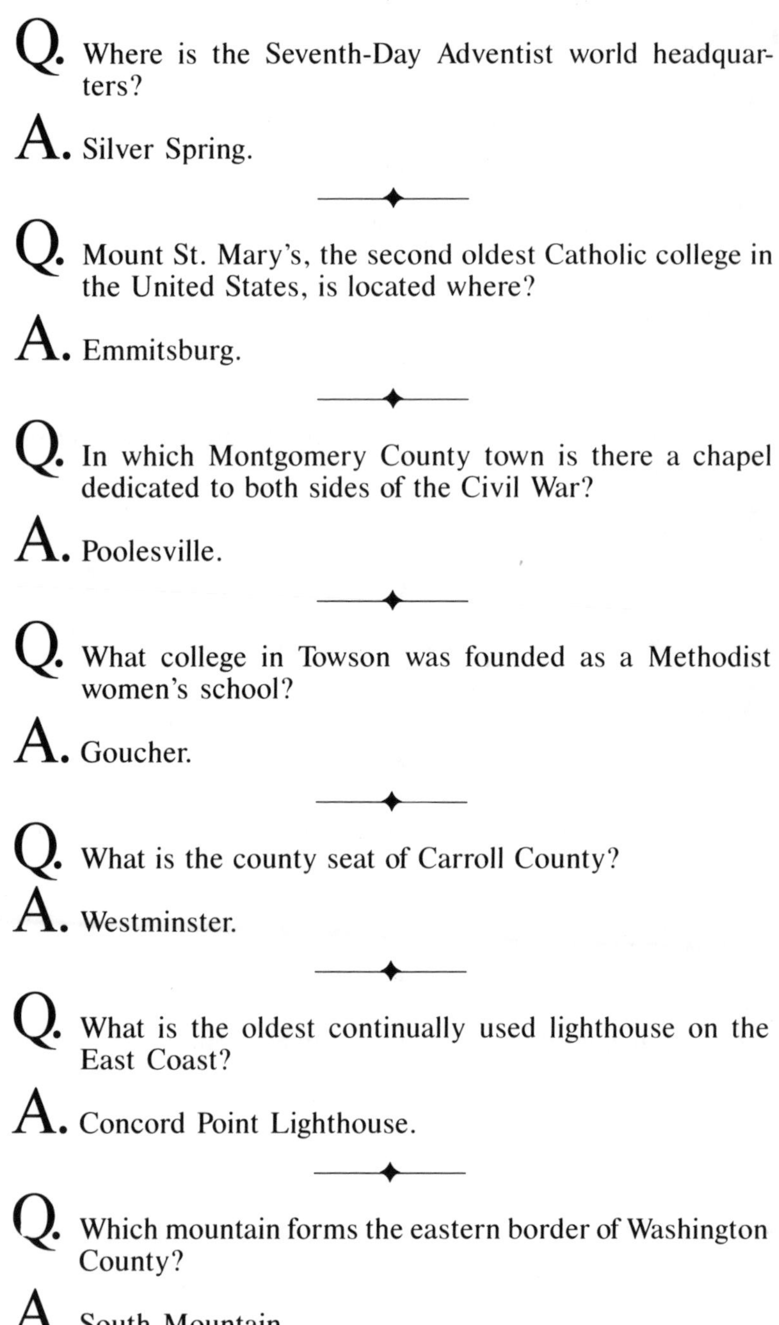

Q. Where is the Seventh-Day Adventist world headquarters?

A. Silver Spring.

Q. Mount St. Mary's, the second oldest Catholic college in the United States, is located where?

A. Emmitsburg.

Q. In which Montgomery County town is there a chapel dedicated to both sides of the Civil War?

A. Poolesville.

Q. What college in Towson was founded as a Methodist women's school?

A. Goucher.

Q. What is the county seat of Carroll County?

A. Westminster.

Q. What is the oldest continually used lighthouse on the East Coast?

A. Concord Point Lighthouse.

Q. Which mountain forms the eastern border of Washington County?

A. South Mountain.

Q. Where is the historic Hotel Gunter?

A. Frostburg.

Q. What are the two southernmost counties on the Eastern Shore?

A. Somerset and Worcester.

Q. On what river is Baltimore situated?

A. Patapsco.

Q. Which county has the highest percentage of college graduates in its population?

A. Montgomery.

Q. Which Baltimore cemetery has a Holocaust Memorial?

A. Mickro Kodesh Beth Israel.

Q. Annapolis is the county seat of which county?

A. Anne Arundel.

Q. What small town in Montgomery County was an early stronghold of the Quakers?

A. Sandy Spring.

Q. In which Maryland city was the first YMCA building in the United States erected in 1859?

A. Baltimore.

Q. Rising Sun is a town in which county?

A. Cecil.

Q. In which Maryland town was America's first Presbyterian church established in 1684?

A. Snow Hill.

Q. Clara Barton, founder of the American Red Cross, operated the organization in which Montgomery County town?

A. Glen Echo.

Q. Which mountain rises above the Monocacy Valley?

A. Sugar Loaf.

Q. What stylish Baltimore neighborhood, designed by Frederick Law Olmstead, Jr., celebrated its 100th birthday in 1991?

A. Roland Park.

Q. Where is the U.S. Naval Ordnance Station?

A. Indian Head.

Q. On what island are the towns of Ewell, Rhodes Point, and Tylerton located?

A. Smith.

Q. What river originates in the Great Cypress Swamp and flows west to the Chesapeake Bay?

A. Pocomoke.

Q. To whom did Maryland give land in 1791?

A. Congress, for the District of Columbia.

Q. What is the official name of the Chesapeake Bay Bridge?

A. William Preston Lane, Jr., Memorial Bridge.

Q. Hagerstown is the county seat of which county?

A. Washington.

Q. What elegant Baltimore neighborhood is often compared to Boston's Beacon Hill?

A. Bolton Hill.

Q. What county has a town called Accident?

A. Garrett.

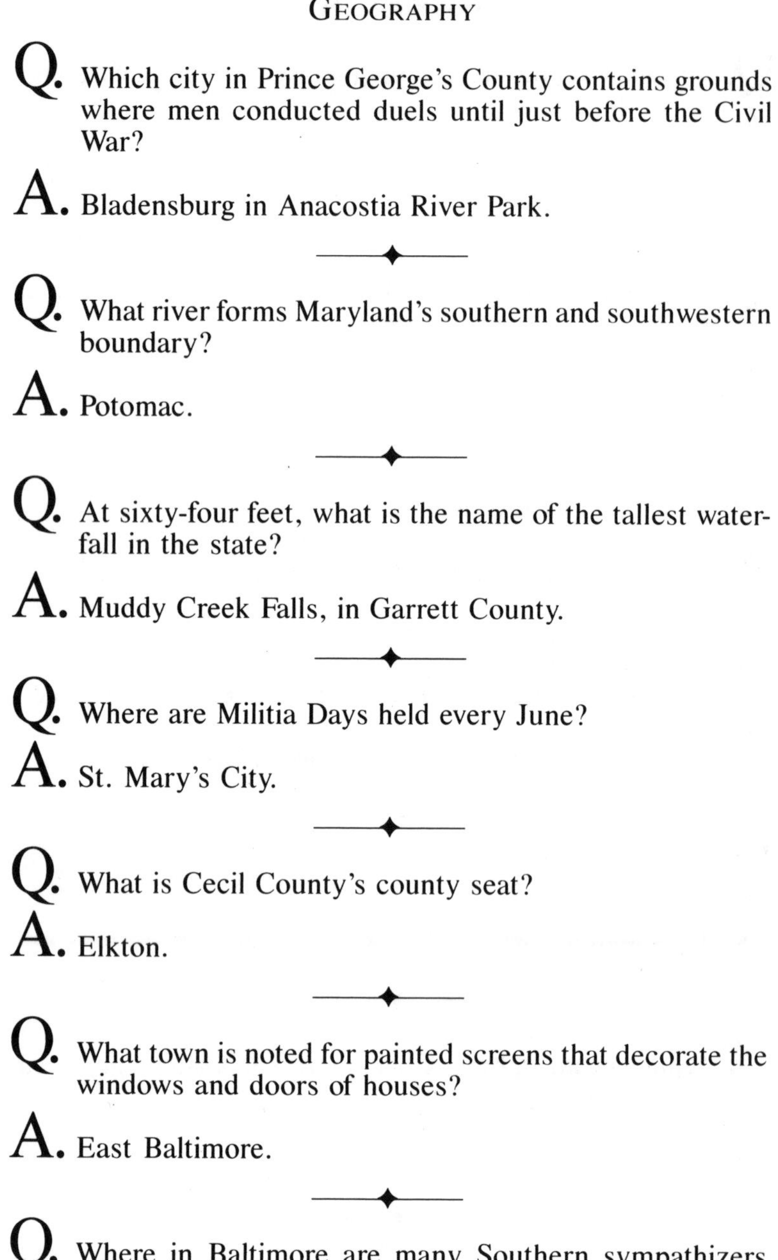

Q. Which city in Prince George's County contains grounds where men conducted duels until just before the Civil War?

A. Bladensburg in Anacostia River Park.

Q. What river forms Maryland's southern and southwestern boundary?

A. Potomac.

Q. At sixty-four feet, what is the name of the tallest waterfall in the state?

A. Muddy Creek Falls, in Garrett County.

Q. Where are Militia Days held every June?

A. St. Mary's City.

Q. What is Cecil County's county seat?

A. Elkton.

Q. What town is noted for painted screens that decorate the windows and doors of houses?

A. East Baltimore.

Q. Where in Baltimore are many Southern sympathizers from Civil War days buried?

A. Confederate Hill at Loudon Park Cemetery.

Q. Where is the refurbished Atlantic Hotel?

A. Berlin.

Q. Where is the Washington Bible College?

A. Lanham.

Q. Ellicott City is the county seat of which county?

A. Howard.

Q. What do Eastern Shore natives call those who live on the east side of the railroad tracks?

A. Sea Siders.

Q. In what county is there a town called Welcome?

A. Charles.

Q. Where is the home base of the Seafarers International Union of North America?

A. Camp Springs.

Q. Which Eastern Shore county has the highest percentage of registered Republicans?

A. Talbot.

Q. In which county does the highest percentage of the labor force work outside the county?

A. Howard.

Q. Where is the Mount Zion One-Room Schoolhouse Museum?

A. Snow Hill.

Q. Which county has the lowest percentage of college graduates?

A. Garrett.

Q. Where is the prestigious Landon School located?

A. Bethesda.

Q. What event is held every August and September in Crownsville?

A. Maryland Renaissance Festival.

Q. What is the Episcopal cathedral in Baltimore called?

A. Cathedral Church of the Incarnation.

Q. Where is the Teackle Mansion?

A. Princess Anne.

Q. Which county has the highest percentage of foreign-born residents?

A. Montgomery.

Q. What is the average cost of a home in Maryland, according to the 1990 census?

A. $116,500.

Q. In which town did Sargent Shriver live when he was a vice-presidential candidate?

A. Rockville.

Q. What is a privy or outhouse called on the Eastern Shore?

A. Back house.

Q. Where is the home base of the Military Chaplains Association of the United States?

A. Riverdale.

Q. What do Eastern Shore folk call a wild youth?

A. Blue hen's chickens.

Q. The World Association of Detectives is headquartered in which Anne Arundel County town?

A. Severna Park.

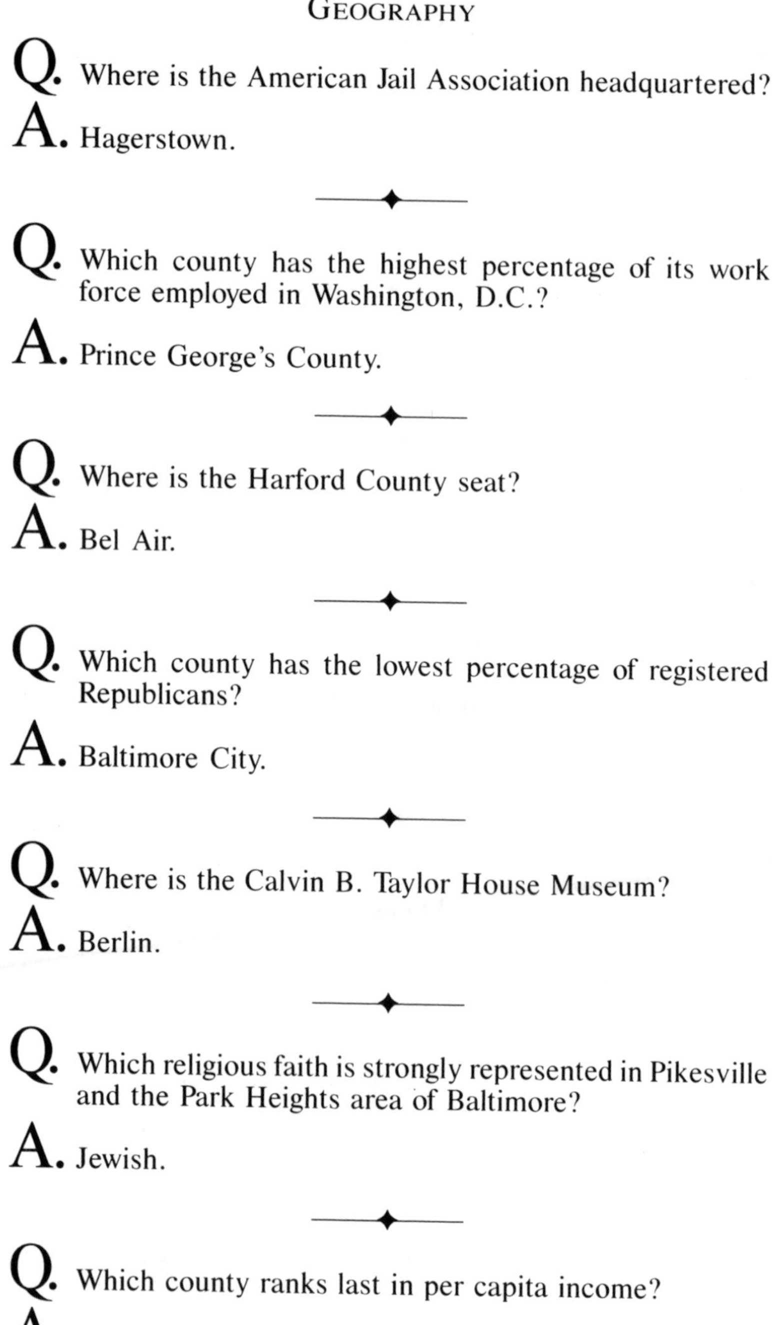

Q. Where is the American Jail Association headquartered?

A. Hagerstown.

Q. Which county has the highest percentage of its work force employed in Washington, D.C.?

A. Prince George's County.

Q. Where is the Harford County seat?

A. Bel Air.

Q. Which county has the lowest percentage of registered Republicans?

A. Baltimore City.

Q. Where is the Calvin B. Taylor House Museum?

A. Berlin.

Q. Which religious faith is strongly represented in Pikesville and the Park Heights area of Baltimore?

A. Jewish.

Q. Which county ranks last in per capita income?

A. Garrett.

Q. In what tiny Montgomery County town is Seven Locks Press?

A. Cabin John.

—♦—

Q. What is a church revival called on the Eastern Shore?

A. Protracted Meeting.

—♦—

Q. Where is the national headquarters of the Phobia Society of America?

A. Rockville.

—♦—

Q. What do Eastern Shore folk call a family dinner?

A. Big Day.

—♦—

Q. Where is the Kent Museum at Turner's Creek?

A. Kennedyville.

—♦—

Q. What do Eastern Shore natives call someone who lives on the west side of the railroad tracks?

A. Bay Sider.

—♦—

Q. What is Allegany County's largest college?

A. Frostburg State University.

Q. Where is the International Taxi Cab Association's home base?

A. Kensington.

—✦—

Q. Which county has the highest percentage of families living below the poverty line?

A. Baltimore City.

—✦—

Q. Which two counties have the highest percentage of students attending private schools?

A. Baltimore and Montgomery.

—✦—

Q. Which county has the lowest percentage of students attending private schools?

A. Somerset.

—✦—

Q. What is the largest county in area?

A. Frederick.

—✦—

Q. The White Swan Tavern is a local history museum in which town?

A. Chestertown.

—✦—

Q. Centreville is the county seat in which Eastern Shore county?

A. Queen Anne's.

Q. In which county do registered Republicans outnumber Democrats by a wide margin?

A. Garrett.

Q. What town is home to the Eastern Shore Early Americana Museum?

A. Marion Station.

Q. What museum at Colton's Point is filled with exhibits about the early residents and settlers in St. Mary's County?

A. Potomac River Museum.

Q. Which county has the highest percentage of people born in Maryland?

A. Dorchester.

Q. The Air Force Sergeant's Association and the National PanHellenic Council are both headquartered where?

A. Temple Hills.

Q. In which county is the Ladew Topiary Gardens?

A. Harford.

Q. Which county has a town called Bethlehem?

A. Caroline.

Q. Where is an American Indian Pow Wow held each July?

A. Garrett County Fairgrounds in McHenry.

Q. What Baltimore County town observes Defenders Day with a reenactment of the 1812 Battle of North Point?

A. Edgemere.

Q. Chestertown is the county seat for which county?

A. Kent.

Q. Where did Kunta Kinte arrive in 1767?

A. Annapolis.

Q. In which Baltimore cemetery are buried twenty-four generals, five commodores, two secretaries of war, three secretaries of the Navy, and thirteen members of Congress?

A. Westminster Burying Ground.

Q. Where does Senator John Glenn live?

A. Potomac.

Q. Pemberton Hall and Popular Hall Mansion are two historical museums located in which town?

A. Salisbury.

Q. Solomon's Island belongs to which county?

A. Calvert.

Q. What is the oldest public building in Maryland?

A. Old Treasury Building in Annapolis.

Q. Which religious shrine stands by Interstate 95, just south of the Elkton exit?

A. Shrine of Our Lady of the Highways.

Q. Where is the Wicomico County seat?

A. Salisbury.

Q. What Episcopal church, situated on the bank of Church Creek, contains a Bible and a Communion chalice given by Queen Anne?

A. Old Trinity Church.

Q. Where is the World Future Society headquartered?

A. Bethesda.

Q. Where is the only existing British stone fort of the colonial period in the United States?

A. Fort Frederick, near Big Pool.

Q. What was the original name of Ellicott City?

A. Ellicott's Mills.

Q. What Democratic bigwig and FDR ally lived in Oxon Hill?

A. Sumner Welles.

Q. Which Catholic cemetery in Baltimore is commonly called "Bonnie Brae"?

A. New Cathedral Cemetery.

Q. Which Baltimore County town had a Confederate Veterans Home until 1932?

A. Pikesville.

Q. Consisting of 365 acres and over 200,000 graves, what is Baltimore's largest cemetery?

A. Loudon Park.

Q. Where is the Somerset County seat?

A. Princess Anne.

Q. What resource, located in Cumberland, provides information on all activities and agencies of the federal government?

A. Federal Information Center.

Q. In which town is the Poultry Hall of Fame?

A. Beltsville.

Q. What is a person not born on the Eastern Shore called?

A. Come Here.

Q. Near what small town in Baltimore County was scientist Benjamin Banneker born?

A. Oella.

Q. What is the name of the Prince George's County military installation where the president's plane takes off and lands?

A. Andrews Air Force Base.

Q. Where is Montpelier Mansion?

A. Laurel.

Q. Denton is which county's county seat?

A. Caroline.

Q. Which county houses the oldest courthouse in continuous use in Maryland?

A. Queen Anne's.

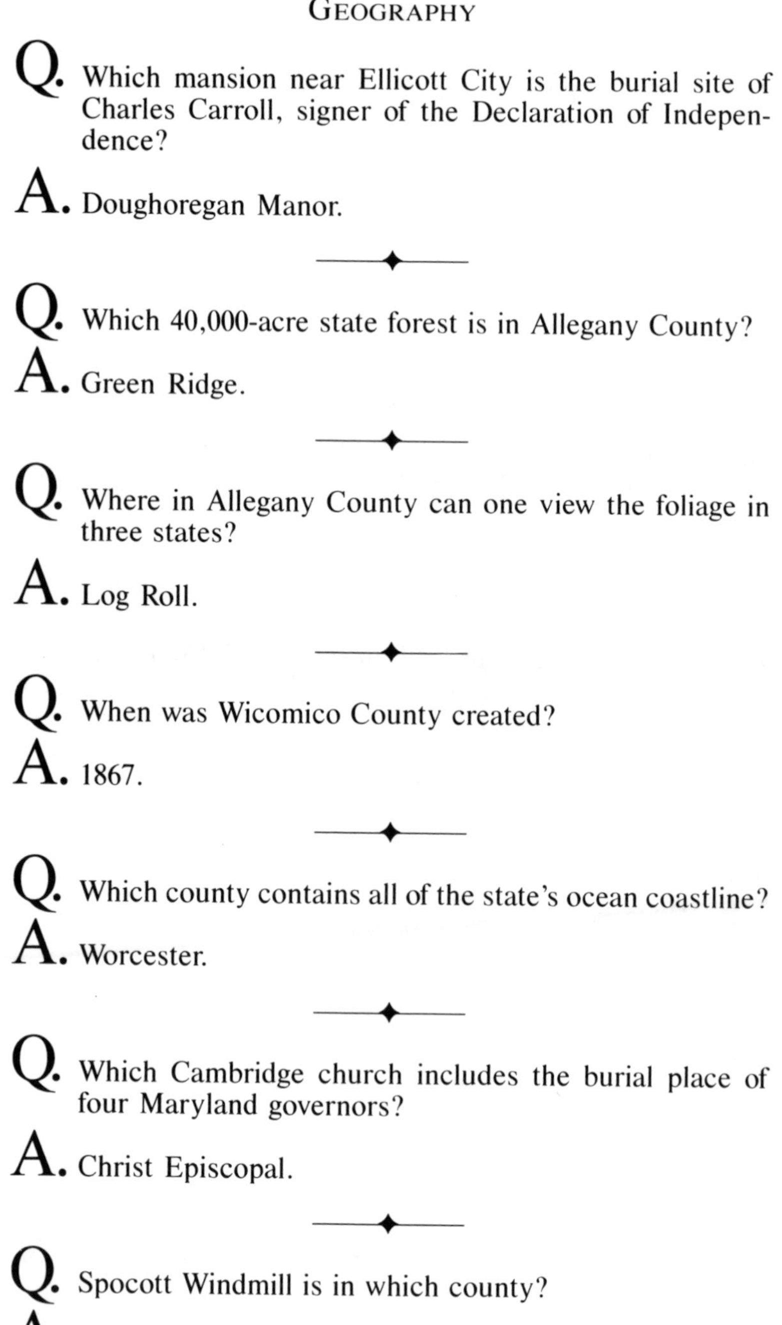

Q. Which mansion near Ellicott City is the burial site of Charles Carroll, signer of the Declaration of Independence?

A. Doughoregan Manor.

Q. Which 40,000-acre state forest is in Allegany County?

A. Green Ridge.

Q. Where in Allegany County can one view the foliage in three states?

A. Log Roll.

Q. When was Wicomico County created?

A. 1867.

Q. Which county contains all of the state's ocean coastline?

A. Worcester.

Q. Which Cambridge church includes the burial place of four Maryland governors?

A. Christ Episcopal.

Q. Spocott Windmill is in which county?

A. Dorchester.

Q. What Allegany County location was used by Union soldiers to monitor Confederate troop movements?

A. Point Lookout.

Q. An Olde Towne Day celebration is now an annual event in which Montgomery County town?

A. Gaithersburg.

Q. Allegany County's seat is where?

A. Cumberland.

Q. How many Maryland governors are buried in Green Mount Cemetery?

A. Nine.

Q. Which founder of the United Brethren in Christ is buried at a historic Baltimore church named for him?

A. Philip Otterbein.

Q. Where does the Blessing of the Fleet take place in October?

A. St. Clements Island.

Q. What county is known as the "Heart of Chesapeake Country" because of its heart shape?

A. Dorchester County.

Q. The county seat of Frederick County is in which town?

A. Frederick.

Q. What town has a historic district called Newtown?

A. Salisbury.

Q. Which river winds through Snow Hill?

A. Pocomoke.

Q. Which town is situated at the confluence of the Tred Avon and Choptank Rivers?

A. Oxford.

Q. Which state park forms the boundary between Caroline and Queen Anne's counties?

A. Tuckahoe.

Q. On which river is Georgetown situated?

A. Sassafras.

Q. Oakland is the county seat for which westernmost county?

A. Garrett.

Q. What is the new area code for Baltimore and the Eastern Shore?

A. 410.

Q. What renowned trial attorney lived in the Tulip Hill section of Bethesda?

A. Edward Bennett Williams.

Q. Which Baltimore cemetery contains the remains of over 200 Methodist preachers?

A. Mount Olivet.

Q. Easton is the county seat for which county?

A. Talbot.

Q. What overlook in Allegany County affords a panoramic view of the surrounding region?

A. Dan's Rock.

Q. Harriet Tubman grew up in which county?

A. Dorchester.

Q. What highly regarded private school, once run by the Sacred Heart nuns, is on Rockville Pike in Bethesda?

A. Stone Ridge School.

Q. Leonardtown is the county seat for which county?

A. St. Mary's.

Q. The Sweet Potato Council of the United States is headquartered in which town?

A. McHenry.

Q. Which county ranks first in per capita income?

A. Montgomery.

Q. Where is the Adkins Historical Museum?

A. Mardela Springs.

Q. If a woman is "gone to Canaan" in Eastern Shore dialect, what does it mean?

A. She is pregnant.

Q. Students living on which island take a "school bus boat" to Crisfield every day?

A. Smith.

Q. What is the name of the Adventist college in Takoma Park?

A. Columbia Union.

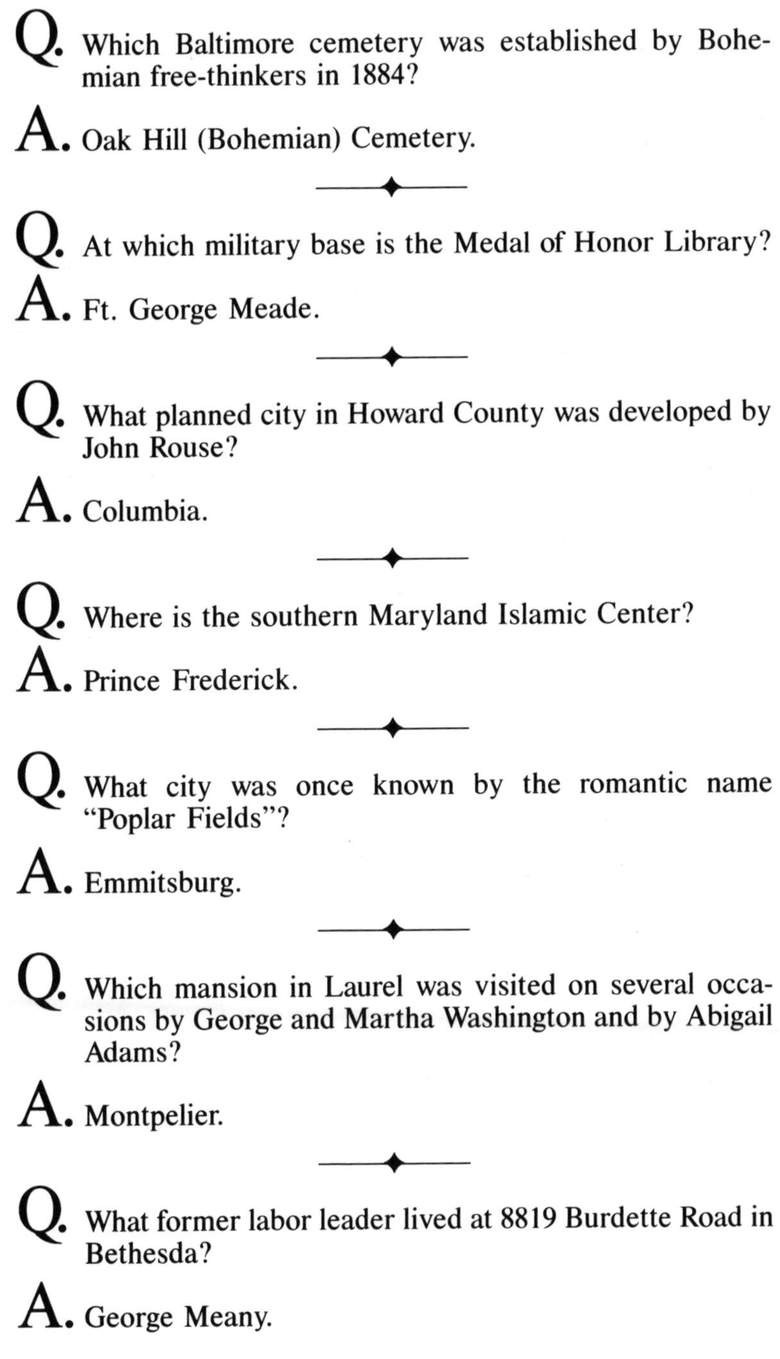

Q. Which Baltimore cemetery was established by Bohemian free-thinkers in 1884?

A. Oak Hill (Bohemian) Cemetery.

Q. At which military base is the Medal of Honor Library?

A. Ft. George Meade.

Q. What planned city in Howard County was developed by John Rouse?

A. Columbia.

Q. Where is the southern Maryland Islamic Center?

A. Prince Frederick.

Q. What city was once known by the romantic name "Poplar Fields"?

A. Emmitsburg.

Q. Which mansion in Laurel was visited on several occasions by George and Martha Washington and by Abigail Adams?

A. Montpelier.

Q. What former labor leader lived at 8819 Burdette Road in Bethesda?

A. George Meany.

Q. Where was Cokesbury College, the first Methodist college in the world, established on June 5, 1785?

A. Abingdon in Harford County.

Q. What woman, called the Moses of her people, was born in a slave cabin near Bucktown?

A. Harriet Tubman.

Q. Where does ABC news political director Hal Bruno live?

A. Chevy Chase.

Q. What general of the army lived with his first wife in Owings Mills from 1925 to 1928?

A. Douglas MacArthur.

Q. Which U.S. vice president lived at 3216 Coquelin Terrace in Chevy Chase?

A. Hubert Humphrey.

Q. Where is the Julia Purnell Museum?

A. Snow Hill.

Q. Where is the Upper Bay Museum?

A. North East.

ENTERTAINMENT

C H A P T E R T W O

Q. What 1947 movie starring George Raft, Randolph Scott, and Joan Blondell was filmed partly in Germantown?

A. *Christmas Eve.*

✦

Q. The 1986 thriller *Bedroom Window* was filmed in which city?

A. Baltimore.

✦

Q. After Virginia coined the slogan "Virginia is for Lovers," what slogan did Maryland adopt?

A. "Maryland is for Crabs."

✦

Q. Where did veteran character actor John Glover grow up?

A. Salisbury.

✦

Q. Fats Waller owned which legendary theater on Pennsylvania Avenue in Baltimore?

A. Royal Theatre.

Q. In which town did actress Goldie Hawn spend her youth?

A. Takoma Park.

Q. What slogan about Maryland did the National Brewing Company promote in the 1950s?

A. "The Land of Pleasant Living."

Q. Which noted nineteenth-century actor was born in Bel Air?

A. Edwin Booth.

Q. Where is the Harlequin Dinner Theatre?

A. Rockville.

Q. What is the name of the music celebration held annually on the banks of Lake Habeeb?

A. The Rocky Gap Festival.

Q. What is the name of Howard County's outdoor entertainment center?

A. Merriweather Post Pavilion.

Q. Who starred in the movie *Clara's Heart*, which was filmed in Baltimore?

A. Whoopi Goldberg.

Q. Where is the Cloister Children's Museum?

A. Brooklandville.

⸻◆⸻

Q. What is the name of the once-famous amusement park high atop South Mountain that was created by the Western Maryland Railroad in 1878 and was reopened as a park in 1977?

A. Pen Mar Park.

⸻◆⸻

Q. The Normandie Farm Inn is a popular "country French" restaurant in which Montgomery County town?

A. Potomac.

⸻◆⸻

Q. What Baltimore stripper fell in love with Gov. Earl K. Long of Louisiana?

A. Blaze Starr.

⸻◆⸻

Q. Which 1979 film featured Al Pacino as a lawyer who single-handedly battled the Maryland judicial system?

A. *And Justice for All.*

⸻◆⸻

Q. Where is the state's official summer theater?

A. Olney.

⸻◆⸻

Q. In which Frederick County town is the Blue Fox Inn?

A. Urbana.

Q. What actor, born in Baltimore in 1930, played Gomez Addams on the "Addams Family"?

A. John Astin.

—✦—

Q. Who was the Baltimore-born romantic hero of silent films who starred in the 1926 version of *Ben Hur*?

A. Francis X. Bushman.

—✦—

Q. Which 1990 film, directed by Barry Levinson and starring Aidin Quinn, was filmed in the Baltimore area?

A. *Avalon*.

—✦—

Q. Which Baltimorean is considered the world's best harmonica player?

A. Larry Adler.

—✦—

Q. Which restaurant in North Beach has been serving Italian food for over fifty years?

A. Franchi's.

—✦—

Q. Which park in Upper Marlboro holds a winter Festival of Lights?

A. Watkins Regional.

—✦—

Q. Which town boasts a Decoy Festival each spring?

A. Havre de Grace.

Q. Which comic actor, born in Baltimore in 1915, played Uncle Tonoose on television's "Make Room for Daddy"?

A. Hans Conreid.

✦

Q. Which Baltimore-born actress won an Oscar for her role in *Death of a Salesman* in 1952?

A. Mildred Dunnock.

✦

Q. The 1988 suspense film *Her Alibi*, which was filmed in Baltimore, starred Paulina Porizkova and what male lead?

A. Tom Selleck.

✦

Q. What "First Lady of Song" worked for a time with Chick Webb in Baltimore?

A. Ella Fitzgerald.

✦

Q. Who was the Baltimorean who founded the rock group Mothers of Invention in 1964?

A. Frank Zappa.

✦

Q. Which bandleader, who often played the White House, was born in Ellicott City in 1895?

A. Meyer Davis.

✦

Q. Who won an Oscar for her role in the Baltimore-based film *Accidental Tourist*?

A. Geena Davis.

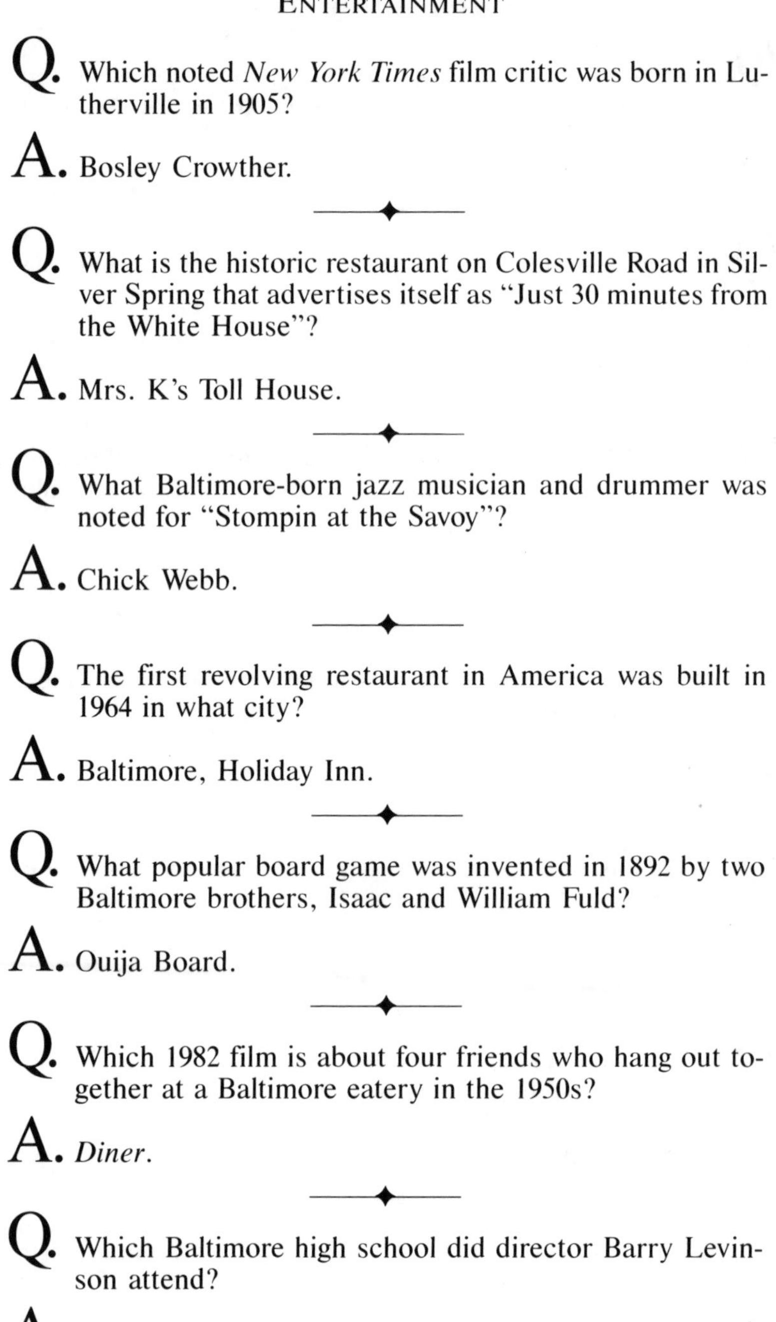

Q. Which noted *New York Times* film critic was born in Lutherville in 1905?

A. Bosley Crowther.

◆

Q. What is the historic restaurant on Colesville Road in Silver Spring that advertises itself as "Just 30 minutes from the White House"?

A. Mrs. K's Toll House.

◆

Q. What Baltimore-born jazz musician and drummer was noted for "Stompin at the Savoy"?

A. Chick Webb.

◆

Q. The first revolving restaurant in America was built in 1964 in what city?

A. Baltimore, Holiday Inn.

◆

Q. What popular board game was invented in 1892 by two Baltimore brothers, Isaac and William Fuld?

A. Ouija Board.

◆

Q. Which 1982 film is about four friends who hang out together at a Baltimore eatery in the 1950s?

A. *Diner*.

◆

Q. Which Baltimore high school did director Barry Levinson attend?

A. Forest Park.

Q. The tawdry and slightly wicked section of Baltimore noted for striptease nightclubs was called what?

A. The Block.

Q. The Province is a popular restaurant in which town?

A. Frederick.

Q. Which Baltimore-born actor had starring roles in "The Young and the Restless" and "Knight Rider"?

A. David Hasselhoff.

Q. What actress, born in Baltimore in 1908, was nominated for an Oscar for her performance in *Barefoot in the Park*?

A. Mildred Natwick.

Q. What Maryland-born journalist was the first woman to anchor a nighttime network newscast?

A. Catherine Mackin.

Q. Which Baltimore-born actor played A. J. Simon on "Simon and Simon"?

A. Jameson Parker.

Q. What state park is six miles east of Cumberland?

A. Rocky Gap.

Q. Which town has a shop called Christmas on the Green?

A. Hagerstown.

Q. What is the popular German-American dining establishment on Baltimore's east side, noted for its paintings as well as its food?

A. Hausner's.

Q. Which bow-tied, crew-cut comedian and Maryland native had a popular CBS variety show from 1958 to 1967?

A. Garry Moore.

Q. Which member of the Peter, Paul, and Mary trio was born in Baltimore in 1937?

A. Noel Paul Stookey.

Q. What award-winning Spanish restaurant is situated in Baltimore?

A. Tio Pepe.

Q. What 1986 comedy, starring Danny Devito and Richard Dreyfuss, was filmed in Baltimore?

A. *Tin Men.*

Q. What retired CBS anchorman now lives near Annapolis?

A. Walter Cronkite.

Q. Maryland was the last state to abolish what kind of censorship?

A. Film.

—✦—

Q. Who directed the 1980 film *Hairspray* and the 1981 film *Polyester*, both filmed in Maryland?

A. John Waters.

—✦—

Q. Baltimore and Ocean City are the locales for what 1984 romance starring Kevin Kline and Sissy Spacek?

A. *Violets Are Blue*.

—✦—

Q. The 1978 film *The Seduction of Joe Tynan* was filmed partly in which Maryland town?

A. Annapolis.

—✦—

Q. The Museum of Costume in St. Michaels contains pantaloons claimed to be worn by which first lady?

A. Mary Todd Lincoln.

—✦—

Q. What is the name of the St. Mary's County mansion owned by Ben Bradlee and Sally Quinn?

A. Porto Bello.

—✦—

Q. Which town hosts a large nighttime parade called The Alsatia Mummers Parade?

A. Hagerstown.

Q. Where is Sandy Point State Park?

A. Annapolis.

Q. What town hosts the annual Miles River Yacht Club Regatta?

A. St. Michaels.

Q. What ethnic culture is celebrated each year at the McHenry Highland Festival?

A. Scottish.

Q. The Fells Point Maritime Festival is held in conjunction with which June holiday?

A. Flag Day.

Q. What event triples the population of Crisfield every Labor Day weekend?

A. The National Hard Crab Derby and Fair.

Q. According to the *1991 Top Ten Almanac*, which Baltimore restaurant is the seventh busiest in the United States?

A. Phillips at Harborplace.

Q. Which Fells Point theater is said to be the oldest little theater in the country?

A. Vagabond Theatre.

Q. What is the name of Baltimore's only Russian restaurant?

A. Moscow Nights.

Q. Which museum sponsors the annual Baltimore International Film Festival?

A. Baltimore Museum of Art.

Q. What is the main attraction for visitors at Chesapeake Village?

A. Discount outlet shopping.

Q. Where is the Pride in Tobacco Festival held every summer?

A. Leonardtown.

Q. Which southern Maryland town holds an Amish Farmers Market every Wednesday and Saturday?

A. Charlotte Hall.

Q. The town of Great Mills is noted for what old shopping establishment?

A. Cecil's General Store and Old Mill.

Q. What are the 700 and 800 blocks on North Howard Street in Baltimore called?

A. Antique Row.

Q. What culinary event is held in Leonardtown every fall?

A. October Oyster Festival.

Q. Which 1895 Victorian hotel in Berlin schedules an annual Dickens Christmas?

A. Atlantic Hotel.

Q. What Baltimore bar is often called the most famous blue collar tavern in town?

A. Hammerjacks.

Q. Which ABC newsman and host of "Nightline" lives on Glen Mill Road in Potomac?

A. Ted Koppel.

Q. Where did Pat Sajak get married?

A. Annapolis.

Q. Which African-American jazz musician, born in East Baltimore in 1883, dominated the 1920s with such musicals and hit songs as *Shuffle Along* and "I'm Just Wild About Harry"?

A. Eubie Blake.

Q. What is the name of the water amusement park in Largo?

A. Wild World.

Q. Since 1962 the Colonial Highland Gathering has been held annually in which town?

A. Fair Hill.

—♦—

Q. What is the name of the popular ice cream parlor that has served generations of happy folks in Middletown since 1912?

A. Main's Ice Cream.

—♦—

Q. Where did famed sharpshooter Annie Oakley live in Maryland?

A. Cambridge.

—♦—

Q. Which Frederick County town celebrates its heritage with Railroad Renaissance Festival each October?

A. Brunswick.

—♦—

Q. Where is the Susquehanna State Park?

A. Havre de Grace.

—♦—

Q. Where is the fall foliage celebrated with an Autumn Glory Festival every year?

A. Deep Creek Lake.

—♦—

Q. Which Talbot County town celebrates an annual fall festival honoring the watermen and their way of life?

A. Tilghman Island.

Q. Where did novelist and screenwriter Caroline Thompson grow up?

A. Bethesda.

—◆—

Q. What millionaire owns a mansion overlooking the ninth green at Avenel Golf Course in Potomac?

A. J. Willard Marriott, Jr.

—◆—

Q. Where does CNN anchorman Bernard Shaw live?

A. Takoma Park.

—◆—

Q. Antique stores are the major attraction of which street in Kensington?

A. Howard Avenue.

—◆—

Q. Which fruit is honored by a festival every August in Leitersburg?

A. Peach.

—◆—

Q. Steve Guttenberg's wedding in *Diner* takes place at what 150-year-old building on Mount Vernon Place in Baltimore?

A. Engineers Society.

—◆—

Q. Street scenes for the film *Avalon* were filmed on what Baltimore street?

A. Appleton.

Q. What avant-garde film director called Baltimore "Trashtown U.S.A."?

A. John Waters.

Q. Where is the studio of WFTY, Channel 50?

A. Rockville.

Q. What 1989 film starring Jessica Lange was filmed partly in Baltimore?

A. *Men Don't Leave*.

Q. Which Baltimorean directed *Rain Man* and *Good Morning, Vietnam*?

A. Barry Levinson.

Q. What grand old movie house on York Road has a Baltimore Walk of Fame, which commemorates films shot in the city?

A. Senator Theatre.

Q. What historic hotel on East Chase Street in Baltimore has welcomed many film stars over the years?

A. Belvedere.

Q. Which star of many John Waters's movies owned a Baltimore thrift store now called Pink Flamingos?

A. Edith Massey.

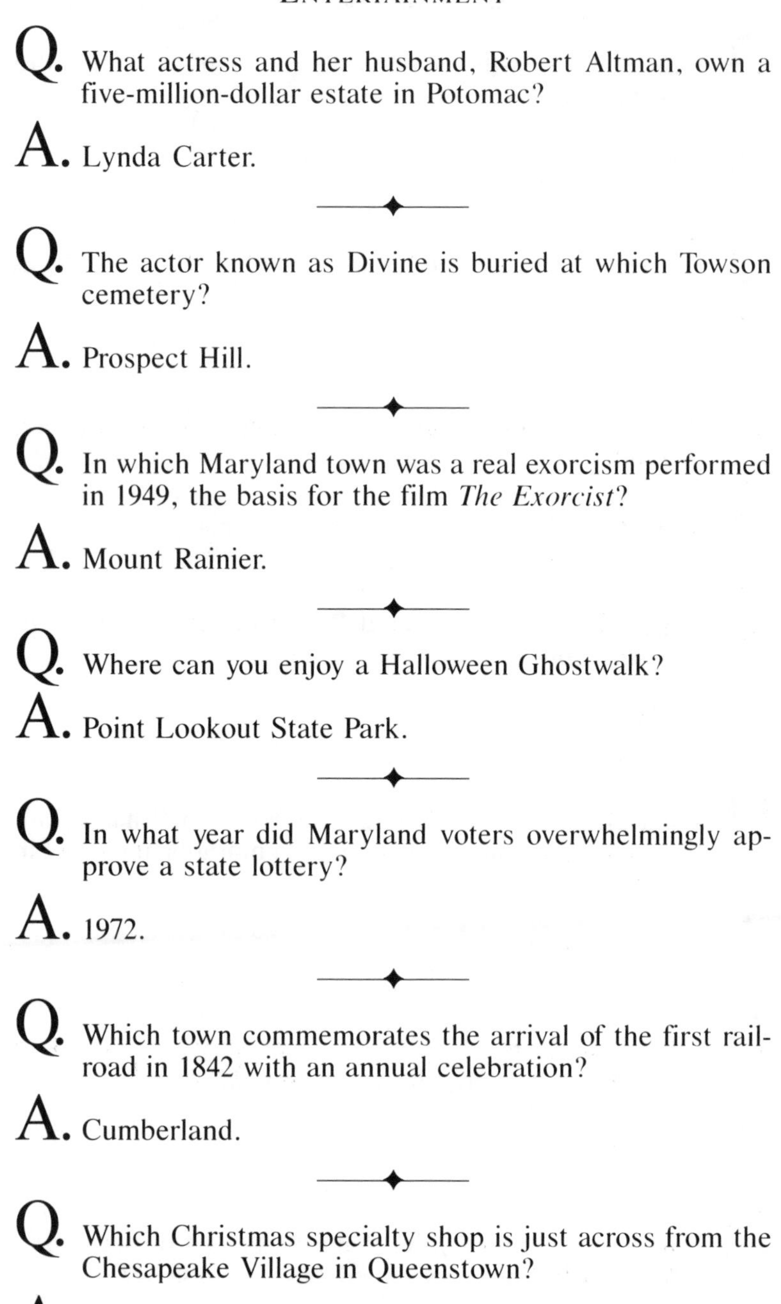

Q. What actress and her husband, Robert Altman, own a five-million-dollar estate in Potomac?

A. Lynda Carter.

Q. The actor known as Divine is buried at which Towson cemetery?

A. Prospect Hill.

Q. In which Maryland town was a real exorcism performed in 1949, the basis for the film *The Exorcist*?

A. Mount Rainier.

Q. Where can you enjoy a Halloween Ghostwalk?

A. Point Lookout State Park.

Q. In what year did Maryland voters overwhelmingly approve a state lottery?

A. 1972.

Q. Which town commemorates the arrival of the first railroad in 1842 with an annual celebration?

A. Cumberland.

Q. Which Christmas specialty shop is just across from the Chesapeake Village in Queenstown?

A. The Christmas Goose, Ltd.

Q. Which town's city park hosts a winter wonderland from Thanksgiving until Epiphany?

A. Salisbury.

—♦—

Q. Legendary stripper Blaze Starr owns a jewelry shop at which Eldersburg location?

A. Carrolltowne Mall.

—♦—

Q. What does Chestertown's Buck Bacchus Museum display?

A. Household articles.

—♦—

Q. Where is *Jazz Times,* "America's Jazz Magazine," published?

A. Silver Spring.

—♦—

Q. How many Marylanders have won the Miss America contest?

A. None.

—♦—

Q. Where can one attend the Maryland Banjo and Fiddle Championships?

A. Autumn Glory Festival at Oakland.

—♦—

Q. Which town celebrates A Taste of Fall Fest?

A. Cumberland.

Q. Where is the Catoctin Colorfest held?

A. Thurmont.

—✦—

Q. Which entertainment center near Ocean City reproduces an Old West town?

A. Frontier Town.

—✦—

Q. The Enchanted Forest theme park is in which county?

A. Howard.

—✦—

Q. What is the name of the barge that brought live entertainment to the isolated small towns of the Chesapeake Bay?

A. James Adams Floating Theatre.

—✦—

Q. What Baltimore-born actor won a Tony nomination for *The Piano Lesson* and now plays the character role in "Roc"?

A. Charles Dutton.

—✦—

Q. Where did Kathie Lee Guiford grow up?

A. Bowie.

—✦—

Q. Which member of the British Royal Family dedicated a statue in Centreville in 1977?

A. Princess Anne.

Q. Which author based her bestselling novel *Show Boat* on a famous Maryland floating theater?

A. Edna Ferber.

—◆—

Q. The Cafe Berlin is an authentic German restaurant in which town?

A. Boonsboro.

—◆—

Q. What winery near Baltimore contains Maryland's oldest vineyards?

A. Boordy Vineyards.

—◆—

Q. Which town hosts an annual day-after-Christmas tour of historic churches and synagogues?

A. Frederick.

—◆—

Q. What has been Maryland's official state slogan in recent years?

A. "Maryland, More Than You Can Imagine."

—◆—

Q. Which county hosts an annual Sheep and Wool Festival?

A. Howard.

—◆—

Q. Which Boonsboro restaurant was occupied by Confederate general D. H. Hill during the Battle of South Mountain?

A. Old South Mountain Inn.

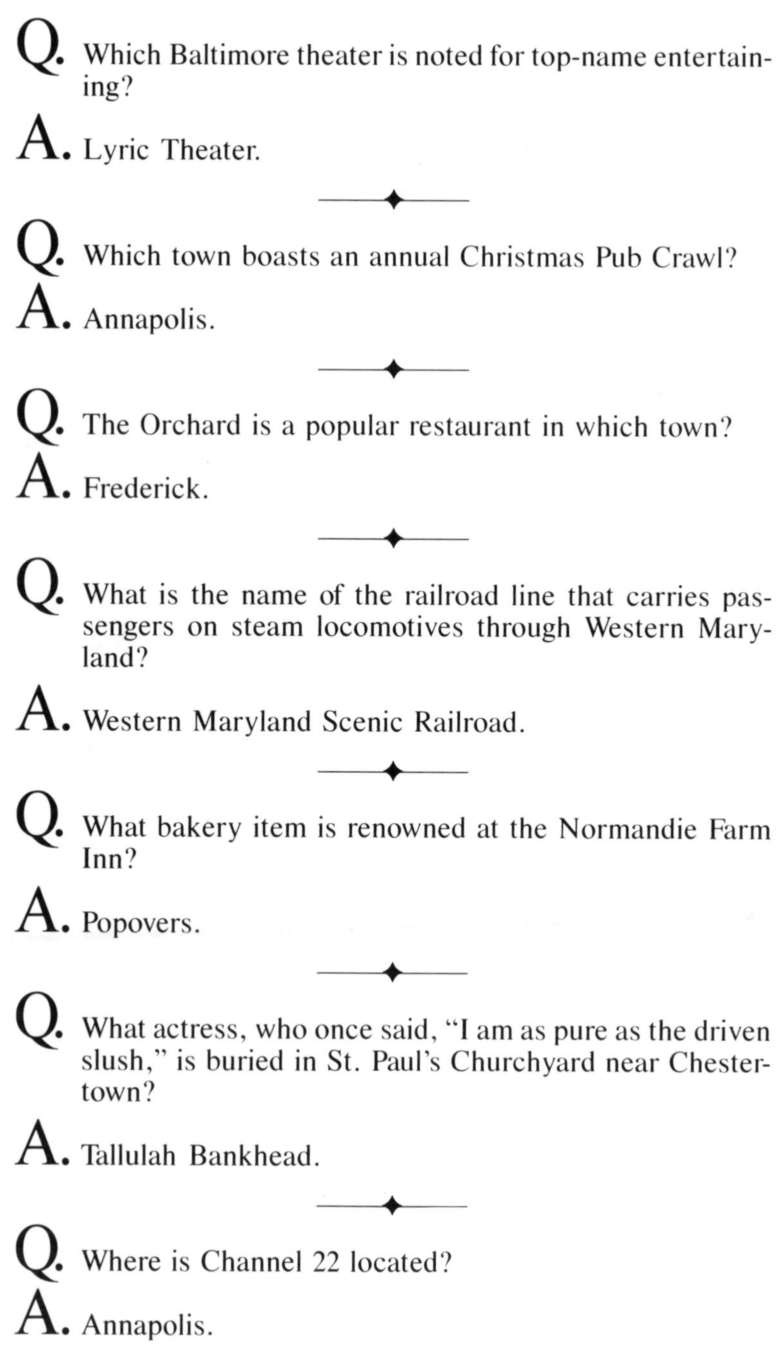

Q. Which Baltimore theater is noted for top-name entertaining?

A. Lyric Theater.

Q. Which town boasts an annual Christmas Pub Crawl?

A. Annapolis.

Q. The Orchard is a popular restaurant in which town?

A. Frederick.

Q. What is the name of the railroad line that carries passengers on steam locomotives through Western Maryland?

A. Western Maryland Scenic Railroad.

Q. What bakery item is renowned at the Normandie Farm Inn?

A. Popovers.

Q. What actress, who once said, "I am as pure as the driven slush," is buried in St. Paul's Churchyard near Chestertown?

A. Tallulah Bankhead.

Q. Where is Channel 22 located?

A. Annapolis.

Q. Which dinner theater is located in Burtonsville?

A. Burn Brae Dinner Theatre.

Q. Which Westminster restaurant was occupied by Confederate troops in 1863?

A. Cockey's Tavern.

Q. Which Baltimore theater is often called The Center for the Performing Arts?

A. Mechanic Theatre.

Q. The original Harford County Courthouse was the site of the first theatrical performance of which famous Shakespearean actor?

A. Edwin Booth.

Q. Where is the Weinberg Center for Performing Arts?

A. Frederick.

Q. Which Thurmont restaurant was inundated by Soviets when Premier Brezhnev visited Camp David in 1979?

A. Cozy Restaurant.

Q. Which entertainment center opened in Baltimore in 1981?

A. Meyerhoff Symphony Hall.

Q. How many Christmas cards are stamped each yuletide at the tiny post office in Bethlehem, Maryland?

A. 80,000.

Q. What former Berlin movie theater, opened around 1910, is now a small shopping mall?

A. Old Globe Theatre.

Q. Which town has a shopping district called Shab Row?

A. Frederick.

Q. Which town holds an annual Festival of Trees?

A. Easton.

Q. Which Baltimore-born singer of jazz and swing was noted for her expressive delivery of songs like "He's Funny That Way"?

A. Billie Holiday.

Q. Where is the "Our Gang" dog, with the ring around his eye, buried?

A. Aspen Hill Pet Cemetery in Wheaton.

Q. What delicacy has become almost a culinary symbol of Maryland?

A. Crab cakes.

HISTORY

CHAPTER THREE

Q. When is Maryland Day?

A. March 25.

Q. What presidential assassin is buried in Baltimore's Green Mount Cemetery?

A. John Wilkes Booth.

Q. Which Maryland town was the site of the bloodiest Civil War battle?

A. Antietam, where over 23,000 soldiers died in one day.

Q. What Revolutionary War hero is buried in the chapel at the U.S. Naval Academy?

A. John Paul Jones.

Q. Maryland was originally founded as a refuge for what religious group?

A. Catholics.

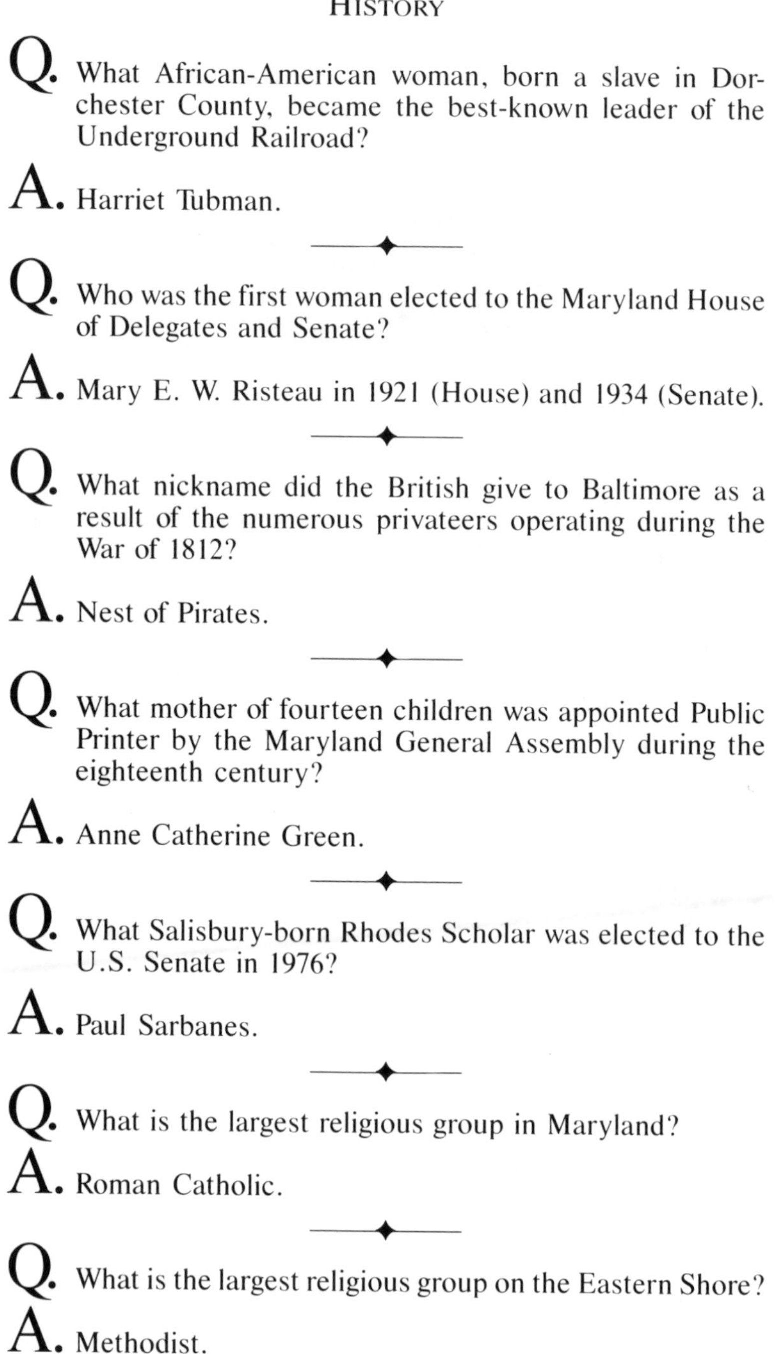

Q. What African-American woman, born a slave in Dorchester County, became the best-known leader of the Underground Railroad?

A. Harriet Tubman.

Q. Who was the first woman elected to the Maryland House of Delegates and Senate?

A. Mary E. W. Risteau in 1921 (House) and 1934 (Senate).

Q. What nickname did the British give to Baltimore as a result of the numerous privateers operating during the War of 1812?

A. Nest of Pirates.

Q. What mother of fourteen children was appointed Public Printer by the Maryland General Assembly during the eighteenth century?

A. Anne Catherine Green.

Q. What Salisbury-born Rhodes Scholar was elected to the U.S. Senate in 1976?

A. Paul Sarbanes.

Q. What is the largest religious group in Maryland?

A. Roman Catholic.

Q. What is the largest religious group on the Eastern Shore?

A. Methodist.

Q. Who was Maryland's first Jewish governor?

A. Marvin Mandel.

Q. Where did George Washington resign his commission as commander in chief of the Continental Army?

A. Maryland State House, in the Old Senate Chamber.

Q. For what crime was one-time Port Tobacco resident George Atzerodt hanged?

A. For his role in Lincoln's assassination.

Q. Maryland's Belle Boyd was a spy for which side during the Civil War?

A. Confederacy.

Q. Which University of Maryland president was a political powerhouse during the 1940s and 1950s?

A. Harry C. ("Curley") Byrd.

Q. In the 1790s, all Maryland governors belonged to which political party?

A. Federalist.

Q. Which Maryland governor nominated Gen. Dwight Eisenhower for president at the 1952 Republican Convention?

A. Theodore McKeldin.

Q. On what train was Lincoln riding on the way to deliver his Gettysburg Address?

A. Western Maryland Railway, which ran until 1927.

Q. For what is Maryland statesman Charles Carroll of Carrollton known?

A. He was the last surviving signer of the Declaration of Independence.

Q. Which Marylander served as secretary of war under Presidents Washington and Adams?

A. James McHenry.

Q. What was the name of the early turnpike that connected Baltimore to Wheeling, West Virginia?

A. National Road.

Q. For which English queen was Maryland named?

A. Henrietta Maria.

Q. What Pennsylvania-German religious group settled near Grantsville and Bittinger in Garrett County in the eighteenth century?

A. Amish.

Q. Which popular men's fraternal order was founded in Baltimore on April 26, 1819?

A. Independent Order of Odd Fellows.

Q. Which daughter of Johns Hopkins University's first president became a prominent socialist and pacifist and ran for governor and U.S. senator?

A. Elizabeth ("Miss Lizzie") Colt Gilman.

Q. What is Maryland's highest state court?

A. Court of Appeals.

Q. What percentage of Marylanders work for the government?

A. 20 percent.

Q. What Maryland-born aide to George Washington carried the message of Cornwallis's surrender at Yorktown to the Continental Congress at Philadelphia?

A. Col. Tench Tilghman.

Q. Which Talbot County senator tried to filibuster against the Chesapeake Bay Bridge?

A. Henry Herbert Balch.

Q. Originally, what was Maryland's only state school that welcomed black students?

A. Bowie State Teacher's College, founded in 1867.

Q. Which Charles County man was elected the first president of the United States in congress assembled on November 5, 1781?

A. John Hanson.

Q. Which secretary of state under President Harry Truman died in Sandy Spring in 1971?

A. Dean Acheson.

———✦———

Q. At which Maryland Civil War battle did the Union repel the first Confederate invasion of the North?

A. Battle of South Mountain.

———✦———

Q. Whom did the Democrats nominate for president in 1912 at their convention in Baltimore?

A. Woodrow Wilson.

———✦———

Q. Baltimore-born Emily Harris was convicted of what crime in 1978?

A. Kidnapping Patty Hearst in 1974.

———✦———

Q. During which war was George Washington an aide to General Braddock at Fort Cumberland, Maryland?

A. French and Indian War.

———✦———

Q. Which first lady, the only one to be married in the White House, died in Baltimore in 1947?

A. Frances Folsom Cleveland.

———✦———

Q. How many Marylanders fought in the Confederate Army?

A. 22,000.

Q. How many Marylanders fought in the Union Army?

A. 62,000.

Q. What Texas judge, born in Baltimore in 1896, administered the oath of office to President Lyndon Johnson after Kennedy's death?

A. Sarah Hughes.

Q. Which Baltimorean founded Hadassah and died in Jerusalem in 1945?

A. Henrietta Szold.

Q. Although born in Cumberland, where did Catholic bishop James Edward Walsh spend most of his life?

A. In China as a missionary for forty years.

Q. Which native of Rockville served as President Gerald Ford's press secretary?

A. Ron Nessen.

Q. How many seats does Maryland have in the U.S. House of Representatives?

A. Eight.

Q. What Glen Ellen aristocrat led bands of southern guerrillas during the Civil War and wrote an account of the activity called *Four Years in the Saddle*?

A. Harry Gilmor.

Q. During which war was Frederick native Winfield Scott Schley called the "hero of Santiago"?

A. Spanish-American War.

Q. What Baltimore college was the first Catholic college for women established in the United States?

A. College of Notre Dame of Maryland.

Q. Who was the first black woman elected to the state senate?

A. Verda Welcome, in 1963.

Q. Which former governor was convicted and jailed for accepting bribes?

A. Marvin Mandel.

Q. Which U.S. president fled to Caleb Bentley's home in Brookeville after the British burned Washington in 1814?

A. James Madison.

Q. Maryland's Ober Law, passed in 1949, was a loyalty oath for public officials and teachers aimed at what "subversive" group?

A. Communists.

Q. Who saved the town of Georgetown from the British during the War of 1812?

A. Kitty Knight.

Q. What were the names of the two ships that brought Maryland's original settlers?

A. *Ark* and *Dove*.

Q. Who beat Millard Tydings in the bitter 1950 U.S. Senate race?

A. John Marshall Butler.

Q. Since 1948, how many times has Maryland supported the losing candidate for president?

A. Three (Dewey, Humphrey, Carter).

Q. Who was chosen America's first Methodist bishop at the 1784 Christmas Conference in Baltimore?

A. Francis Asbury.

Q. What freedom was guaranteed in the famous 1649 Act of Toleration?

A. Religious freedom.

Q. Under which governor did Maryland enact a Public Accommodations Law to forbid racial discrimination in public places?

A. Millard Tawes.

Q. Which professor at Johns Hopkins University was accused of being a Communist by Senator Joseph McCarthy?

A. Owen Lattimore.

Q. Which normally Democratic county on the Eastern Shore bolted to support Barry Goldwater in 1964?

A. Dorchester.

Q. What was the name of the federal agency that, in the 1940s, employed nearly one-fifth of all the workers in the state?

A. Works Progress Administration.

Q. What famous military hero was killed in a duel in Bladensburg on March 22, 1820?

A. Commodore Stephen Decatur.

Q. Which colonial home in Leonardtown is said to be haunted by the ghost of Joseph Key?

A. Tudor Hall.

Q. Maryland was the only state to support which third party, whose presidential candidate was Millard Fillmore, in 1856?

A. American or Know-Nothing Party.

Q. Who was Maryland's Civil War governor, who tried to keep the state in the Union?

A. Thomas Hicks.

Q. Who was the first Jewish city councilman in Baltimore?

A. Solomon Etting, elected in 1826.

Q. Who carried Maryland in the 1988 presidential election?

A. George Bush.

Q. What perennial Democratic candidate lost to Spiro Agnew in the 1966 governor's race?

A. George Mahoney.

Q. How many electoral votes does Maryland cast in presidential elections?

A. Ten.

Q. Soldiers from which side in the Civil War are buried in the National Cemetery at Antietam?

A. Union.

Q. Which presidential candidate carried every Maryland county in 1956?

A. Dwight D. Eisenhower.

Q. What nineteenth-century evangelist, called the "Parson of the Islands," converted virtually the whole population on Smith Island and nearby communities on the Tangier Sound?

A. Joshua Thomas, who sailed in a log canoe called *The Methodist*.

Q. Which Maryland naval commander was the bane of the British for forty years?

A. Joshua Barney.

Q. What journalist, turned Carroll County farmer, accused Maryland diplomat Alger Hiss of treason?

A. Whittaker Chambers.

Q. What was the only jurisdiction that George McGovern carried in 1972?

A. Baltimore City.

Q. What atheist leader fought compulsory public school prayer when she resided in Baltimore in the late 1950s and early 1960s?

A. Madalyn Murray O'Hair.

Q. The veterans of which war are honored at a memorial that was dedicated on May 28, 1989, in Middle Branch Park in Baltimore City?

A. Vietnam (the Maryland Vietnam Veterans Memorial honors the 1,046 Marylanders who died in that conflict).

Q. Who was the youngest man elected governor of Maryland?

A. Herbert R. O'Conor, age 42.

Q. Which Methodist evangelist was imprisoned during the Revolution for supporting the Tories?

A. Rev. Freeborn Garretson.

Q. During the Civil War, which side did the Eastern Shore favor?

A. Confederacy.

Q. Which English king granted the original charter to Maryland?

A. Charles I.

—✦—

Q. Which Baltimore church became the first black Catholic parish in America in 1863?

A. St. Francis Xavier.

—✦—

Q. What ship, laden with 2,000 pounds of tea, was burned on October 19, 1774 by irate Marylanders?

A. *The Peggy Stewart.*

—✦—

Q. Which political party has always carried Columbia in presidential races?

A. Democratic.

—✦—

Q. What general was entertained at the Fountain Inn in Baltimore while he was on his way to Yorktown?

A. George Washington.

—✦—

Q. What kind of education law did Maryland pass in 1902?

A. Compulsory attendance.

—✦—

Q. Many Maryland churches were financed from what kind of revenue?

A. Lotteries.

Q. Which New Deal personality is honored by a room at the Greenbelt Library?

A. Rexford Guy Tugwell.

Q. What was the name of the papers found on a farm near Westminster that led to the conviction of Maryland diplomat Alger Hiss for treason?

A. Pumpkin Papers.

Q. Which Maryland naval hero fought in Tripoli?

A. Stephen Decatur.

Q. Which Marylander was the U.S. attorney general who prepared the Declaration of War against England in 1812?

A. William Pinkney.

Q. Where did Marylanders suffer a major defeat during the War of 1812?

A. The Battle of Bladensburg.

Q. Who was in command at Fort McHenry during the British assault in the War of 1812?

A. Lt. Col. George Armistead.

Q. Which niece of President Buchanan, who served as first lady during his presidency, is buried in Baltimore?

A. Harriet Lane (Johnston).

Q. What controversial black preacher was raised in Rockville?

A. Father Devine.

Q. Who was the first woman elected to the U.S. Congress from Maryland?

A. Katherine Byron.

Q. Whom did Baltimore honor with a monument in 1792?

A. Christopher Columbus.

Q. Who was nominated for president when the Democrats met in Baltimore in 1832?

A. Andrew Jackson.

Q. Which Polish patriot organized a legion in Baltimore in 1778 to fight for American independence?

A. Gen. Casimir Pulaski.

Q. Who was the hated tax collector appointed to enforce the Stamp Act in Maryland in 1765?

A. Zachariah Hood, who fled the state after being burned in effigy by demonstrators.

Q. Who fought valiantly against the British during their attack on Havre de Grace in 1813?

A. John O'Neil.

Q. Who commanded Maryland troops at the Battle of Long Island?

A. Maj. Mordecai Gist.

Q. Where was America's first railroad station?

A. Mount Clare station in Baltimore, which opened in 1830.

Q. When was the disastrous Baltimore fire?

A. 1904.

Q. What Baltimore publisher established the first postal system in the United States?

A. William Goddard.

Q. Which Marylander was chief justice of the United States when the controversial *Dred Scott* decision was announced?

A. Roger Brooke Taney.

Q. What two occupations are represented by the two men who stand on either side of the Great Seal of Maryland?

A. Farmer and fisherman.

Q. Which Marylander is often called the first woman attorney in the United States?

A. Margaret Brent.

Q. Which Baltimore church is the mother church of American Methodism?

A. Lovely Lane Methodist Church.

Q. What is the state motto as translated in 1975?

A. Manly Deeds, Womanly Words.

Q. Which Confederate general tried to invade Washington, D.C., through the Maryland countryside?

A. Jubal Early.

Q. Which Maryland senator sponsored the bill granting independence to the Philippines?

A. Millard Tydings.

Q. Who was the southern Maryland doctor imprisoned for his alleged involvement in the assassination of Abraham Lincoln?

A. Samuel Mudd.

Q. Which Maryland governor was considered a strong presidential contender in the 1920s and early 1930s?

A. Albert Ritchie.

Q. Who founded the colony of Maryland?

A. Lord Baltimore.

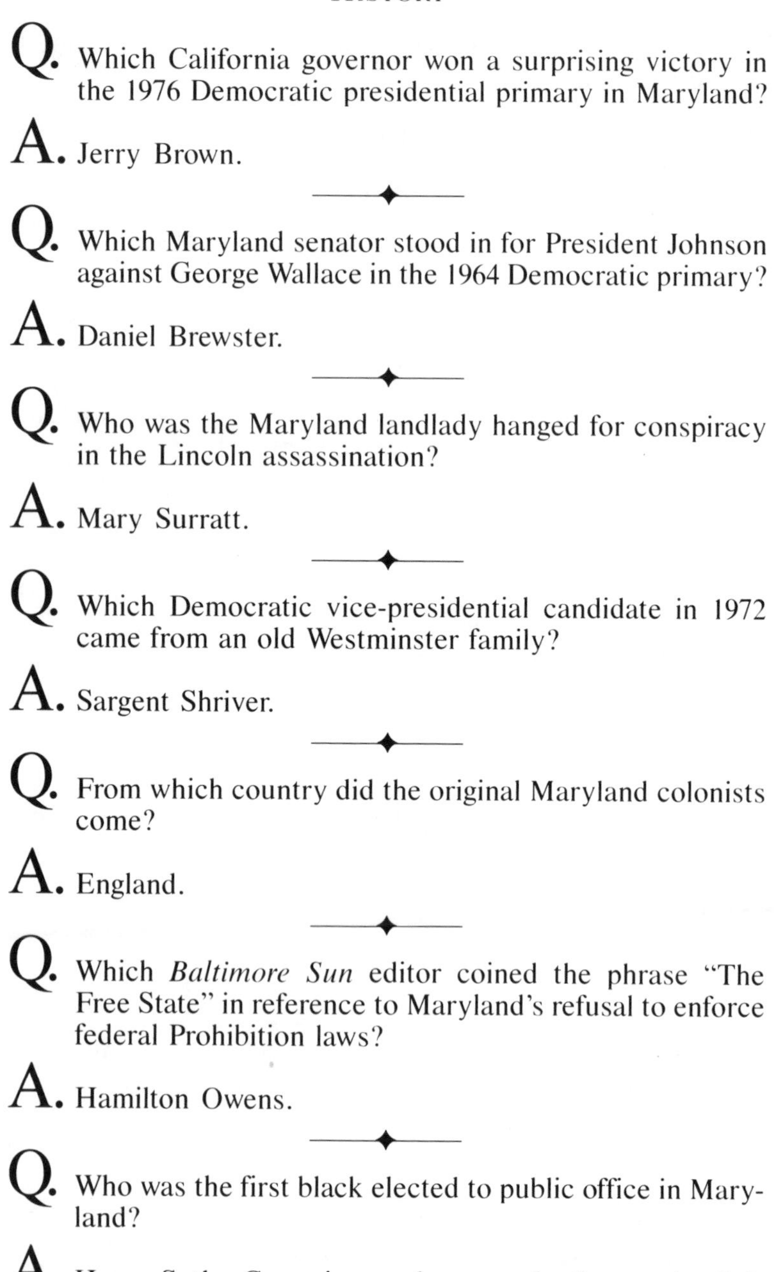

Q. Which California governor won a surprising victory in the 1976 Democratic presidential primary in Maryland?

A. Jerry Brown.

Q. Which Maryland senator stood in for President Johnson against George Wallace in the 1964 Democratic primary?

A. Daniel Brewster.

Q. Who was the Maryland landlady hanged for conspiracy in the Lincoln assassination?

A. Mary Surratt.

Q. Which Democratic vice-presidential candidate in 1972 came from an old Westminster family?

A. Sargent Shriver.

Q. From which country did the original Maryland colonists come?

A. England.

Q. Which *Baltimore Sun* editor coined the phrase "The Free State" in reference to Maryland's refusal to enforce federal Prohibition laws?

A. Hamilton Owens.

Q. Who was the first black elected to public office in Maryland?

A. Harry Sythe Cummings, who won election to the Baltimore City Council in 1890.

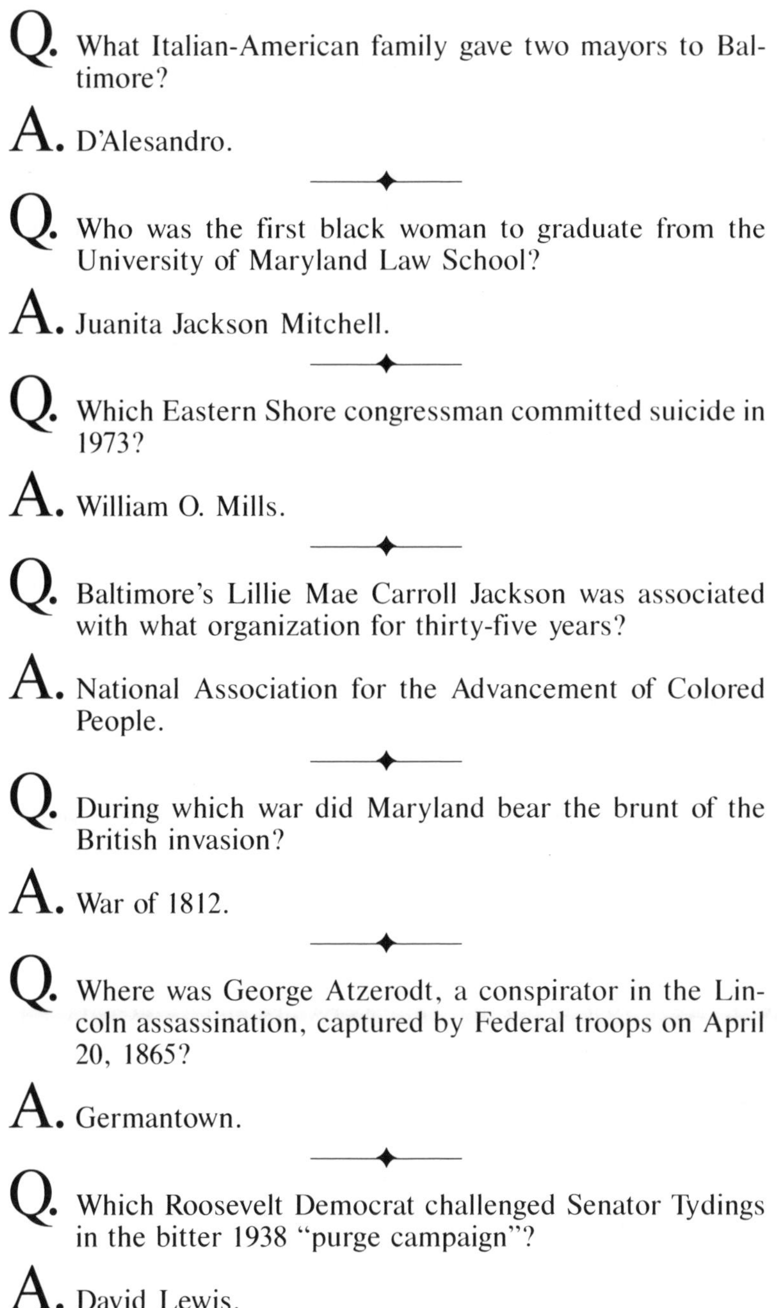

Q. What Italian-American family gave two mayors to Baltimore?

A. D'Alesandro.

Q. Who was the first black woman to graduate from the University of Maryland Law School?

A. Juanita Jackson Mitchell.

Q. Which Eastern Shore congressman committed suicide in 1973?

A. William O. Mills.

Q. Baltimore's Lillie Mae Carroll Jackson was associated with what organization for thirty-five years?

A. National Association for the Advancement of Colored People.

Q. During which war did Maryland bear the brunt of the British invasion?

A. War of 1812.

Q. Where was George Atzerodt, a conspirator in the Lincoln assassination, captured by Federal troops on April 20, 1865?

A. Germantown.

Q. Which Roosevelt Democrat challenged Senator Tydings in the bitter 1938 "purge campaign"?

A. David Lewis.

Q. Citizens of which small town erected a monument to George Washington on South Mountain in 1827?

A. Boonsboro.

Q. Who was the black entrepreneur who founded the Chesapeake Marine Railway and Dry Dock Company?

A. Isaac Myers.

Q. What legal holiday is celebrated in Maryland on September 12?

A. Defenders Day.

Q. In what year did English Quaker George Fox come to Maryland to establish the Society of Friends?

A. 1672.

Q. In which town are several thousand Confederate soldiers buried in Rose Hill Cemetery?

A. Hagerstown.

Q. As of 1990, what percentage of Marylanders owned their own homes?

A. 65 percent, up from 62 percent in 1980.

Q. What Baltimore reformer served as Theodore Roosevelt's attorney general?

A. Charles J. Bonaparte.

Q. What is the name of the first Catholic seminary in America?

A. St. Mary's, in Baltimore.

Q. A fiery sermon by William Ellery Channing in Baltimore in 1819 led to the beginning of what denomination?

A. Unitarian.

Q. Which Bladensburg man was U.S. attorney general and a presidential candidate in 1832?

A. William Wirt.

Q. Which town had an eighteenth-century social club called the Tuesday Club?

A. Annapolis.

Q. Which state nearly fought an oyster war with Maryland in the 1870s and 1880s over boundary lines in the Chesapeake Bay?

A. Virginia.

Q. In 1807, Maryland jurist Luther Martin defended whom of the charge of treason?

A. Aaron Burr.

Q. What Marylander was an associate justice of the Supreme Court when the Senate tried to impeach him?

A. Samuel Chase, who was acquitted.

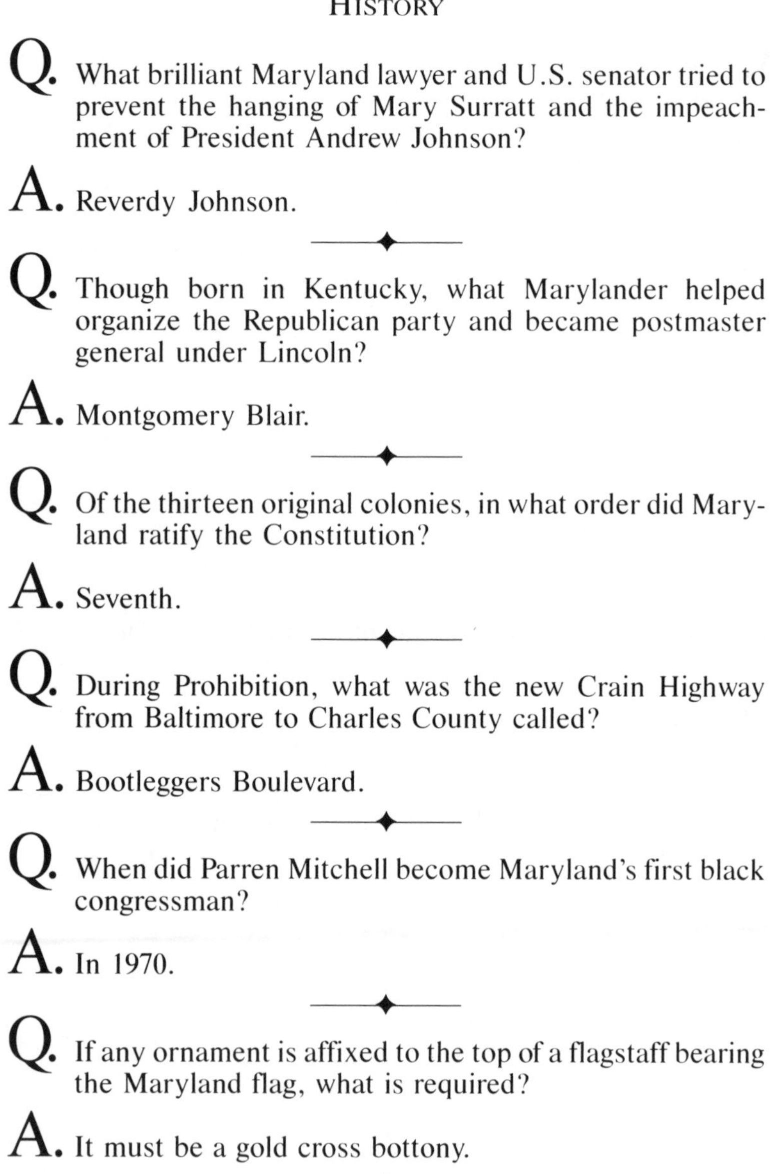

Q. What brilliant Maryland lawyer and U.S. senator tried to prevent the hanging of Mary Surratt and the impeachment of President Andrew Johnson?

A. Reverdy Johnson.

Q. Though born in Kentucky, what Marylander helped organize the Republican party and became postmaster general under Lincoln?

A. Montgomery Blair.

Q. Of the thirteen original colonies, in what order did Maryland ratify the Constitution?

A. Seventh.

Q. During Prohibition, what was the new Crain Highway from Baltimore to Charles County called?

A. Bootleggers Boulevard.

Q. When did Parren Mitchell become Maryland's first black congressman?

A. In 1970.

Q. If any ornament is affixed to the top of a flagstaff bearing the Maryland flag, what is required?

A. It must be a gold cross bottony.

Q. According to the 1990 census, what percentage of Maryland households are traditional married-couple families?

A. 54 percent, down from 59 percent in 1980.

Q. In addition to red and white, what other two colors are found on the state flag?

A. Gold and black.

Q. What Baltimore woman married Napoleon's brother Jerome in 1803?

A. Betsy Patterson.

Q. Which Marylander was the first director of the Peace Corps?

A. Sargent Shriver.

Q. Who was the Hagerstown legislator who fought for equal rights for Jews in the nineteenth century?

A. Thomas Kennedy.

Q. Which political party always carries Garrett County in presidential elections?

A. Republican.

Q. Who was shot and crippled during a presidential campaign appearance in 1972 in a Laurel shopping center?

A. Alabama Gov. George Wallace.

Q. What retired Maryland congressman was once director of the Congressional Research Service at the Library of Congress?

A. Gilbert Gude.

Q. Maryland's William Rogers was which president's attorney general?

A. Dwight Eisenhower.

—♦—

Q. Which political party almost always carries Baltimore City?

A. Democratic.

—♦—

Q. What Maryland governor became U.S. vice president in 1969?

A. Spiro Agnew.

—♦—

Q. Which long-time Republican senator from Maryland retired in 1986?

A. Charles Mathias.

—♦—

Q. Which Baltimore mayor was elected governor in 1986?

A. William Donald Schaefer.

—♦—

Q. In which presidential election were both vice-presidential candidates from Maryland?

A. 1972.

—♦—

Q. Who made the large flag that inspired the "Star Spangled Banner"?

A. Mary Pickersgill.

Q. Which church was established in Maryland by law after 1692?

A. Church of England.

Q. Which Marylander was the first black U.S. Supreme Court justice?

A. Thurgood Marshall.

Q. By what percent did Maryland's population grow from 1980 to 1990?

A. 13.4 percent.

Q. Because of death threats, which president had to sneak through Maryland anonymously on the way to his inauguration?

A. Abraham Lincoln.

Q. What recent first lady lived in Bethesda in her youth?

A. Nancy Reagan.

Q. The bravery of Maryland troops during the Revolution gave the state what nickname?

A. "Old Line State."

Q. What is the largest religious group in Frederick County?

A. Lutheran.

Q. Benjamin Civiletti of Baltimore was attorney general under which president?

A. Jimmy Carter.

Q. Where does Maryland rank among the states in 1990 population?

A. Nineteenth.

Q. Which Eastern Shore congressman served in the cabinets of Nixon and Ford?

A. Rogers Morton.

Q. Which battle was fought in Maryland on July 9, 1864 to prevent a Confederate invasion of Washington, D.C.?

A. Battle of Monocacy.

Q. How did a *National Geographic* writer once describe Maryland?

A. "America in miniature."

Q. Which Civil War battle was fought in Maryland three days before Antietam?

A. Battle of South Mountain.

Q. Henry Kyd Douglas, who lived at Ferry Hill Place in Washington County, served on the staff of what Confederate general?

A. Stonewall Jackson.

Q. When was the Mason-Dixon Line formally adopted?

A. July 4, 1760.

Q. During the Vietnam War, which Baltimore County town was the site of a famous antiwar incident?

A. Catonsville.

Q. Dr. Jacob Lumbroso, a Portuguese physician who arrived in Maryland in 1656, is thought to be the first in what category?

A. The first Jewish resident of Maryland.

Q. Mary K. Goddard was the first person to hold which position in Baltimore?

A. Postmaster, from 1775 to 1790.

Q. What was the first bank in America to pay interest on deposits?

A. Farmer's Bank of Annapolis, in 1805.

Q. Henry Sater's church in Chestnut Ridge was the first congregation of which denomination in Maryland?

A. Baptist.

Q. The first complete Rural Free Delivery service of the U.S. Post Office began in which Maryland county on August 20, 1899?

A. Carroll.

Q. Who became the first governor of Maryland in 1777?

A. Thomas Johnson, Jr.

Q. Approximately what percentage of Marylanders are African Americans?

A. 25 percent.

Q. Who is the Maryland priest who founded a unique Catholic home mission society, The Glenmary Home Missioners, in 1939?

A. Howard Bishop, who was pastor of St. Louis Church in Clarksville from 1917 to 1937.

Q. How many provisions does the Maryland Constitution have in its Bill of Rights?

A. Forty-two, more than any other state.

Q. What former Maryland governor often appeared with a black-eyed Susan in his lapel?

A. Millard Tawes.

Q. What famous world leader accompanied President Franklin Roosevelt for a tour of the Barbara Fritchie House in Frederick?

A. Winston Churchill.

Q. What beloved civil rights advocate in Prince George's County died in 1991?

A. Cora Lee Rice.

Q. Where in Maryland was the largest prison camp of the Civil War located?

A. Point Lookout, where 52,264 Confederate soldiers were imprisoned and more than 3,000 died.

Q. Which signer of the Declaration of Independence owned "Habre de Venture" in Port Tobacco?

A. Thomas Stone.

Q. What was Francis Scott Key's occupation at the time he wrote the national anthem?

A. Lawyer.

Q. How many members are there in the Maryland House of Delegates?

A. 141.

Q. Which revered politician was attorney general under Zachary Taylor?

A. Reverdy Johnson.

Q. Where does Baltimore rank among the nation's cities in 1990 population?

A. Thirteenth.

Q. Who owns the original manuscript of the "Star Spangled Banner"?

A. Maryland Historical Society in Baltimore.

Q. Where does Maryland rank in public school per pupil spending?

A. Sixth.

Q. Which national civil rights organization moved its headquarters from Brooklyn to Baltimore in 1988?

A. National Association for the Advancement of Colored People.

Q. How many members are there in the Maryland State Senate?

A. Forty-seven.

Q. Which church in Baltimore houses a historic 15,000-volume library, with books dating back to 1539?

A. Zion Lutheran Church.

Q. Which two family coats of arms are represented on Maryland's state flag?

A. Calverts and Crosslands.

Q. Which religious order maintains the St. Jude Shrine in Baltimore?

A. Pallotine Fathers.

Q. From which language does the Maryland state motto derive?

A. Italian.

Q. Which former Maryland governor has a historical museum named for him at Somers Cove Marina in Crisfield?

A. Millard Tawes.

Q. For which first lady is a public high school in Prince George's County named?

A. Eleanor Roosevelt.

Q. When does the general assembly begin its annual meeting?

A. Second Wednesday in January.

Q. Who is Maryland's longtime comptroller of the treasury?

A. Louis Goldstein.

Q. Where does Maryland rank among the states in per capita income?

A. Sixth.

Q. Who was elected Maryland's lieutenant governor in 1986?

A. Melvin A. Steinberg.

Q. Which Baltimore Cardinal was actively involved in the civil rights movement in the 1960s?

A. Lawrence Shehan.

Q. How many members are there on the Baltimore City Council?

A. Nineteen.

Q. Who is pictured as a knight on the front of the Maryland State Seal?

A. Lord Baltimore.

Q. When was the first official raising of the fifty-star flag at Fort McHenry?

A. July 4, 1960.

Q. Who were Maryland's four signers of the Declaration of Independence?

A. Charles Carroll, William Paca, Samuel Chase, and Thomas Stone.

Q. Over whose grave in Frederick does the American flag fly day and night?

A. Francis Scott Key.

Q. What percent of Marylanders were born in the state?

A. Fifty-five.

Q. Who was Maryland's first black resident?

A. Mathias de Sousa, who arrived on the *Ark* in 1634.

Q. Which daughter of Robert Kennedy lives in Baltimore County and ran for Congress there in 1986?

A. Kathleen Kennedy Townsend.

Q. What founder of Trinity Church in Upper Marlboro became the first Episcopal bishop consecrated in the United States?

A. Thomas Clagett.

Q. Which English king received one-fifth of the gold and silver found in Maryland?

A. Charles I.

Q. What Annapolis clergyman, though a friend of George Washington, remained loyal to England?

A. Jonathan Boucher.

Q. What religious denomination held a contentious national meeting in Baltimore in 1991?

A. Presbyterian.

Q. For how many days does the state general assembly meet each year?

A. Ninety days.

Q. Which British prime minister has a high school named for him in Potomac?

A. Winston Churchill.

Q. How many Marylanders received the Congressional Medal of Honor during World War II?

A. Four.

Q. Which celebrated abolitionist used Maryland's Samples Manor as his final staging area to attack Harper's Ferry in 1859?

A. John Brown.

Q. What was Maryland's 1990 population?

A. 4,798,622.

Q. For which black Marylander is the Baltimore city courthouse named?

A. Clarence Mitchell.

Q. What is the oldest cruciform, or cross-shaped, church in Maryland?

A. Middleham Chapel, Lusby, in Calvert County (1748).

Q. What Baltimorean became the first woman lawyer licensed to practice in Maryland after the legislature passed a law admitting women to the bar in 1902?

A. Etta Maynie Maddox.

Q. Waverly Mansion, an eighteenth-century home in Marriottsville, was owned by what Maryland governor?

A. George Howard.

Q. During which war did the British Royal Navy and an American flotilla fight the Battle of St. Leonard Creek in Maryland?

A. War of 1812.

Q. When was the U.S. Naval Academy in Maryland founded?

A. 1845.

Q. Whose statue stands on the green in front of the county courthouse in Centreville?

A. Queen Anne.

Q. About what percentage of blacks in Maryland were free in 1860?

A. About 50 percent.

Q. Which Maryland senator was called the "Squire of Oakington"?

A. Millard Tydings.

Q. What French religious order sent many of its priests to Maryland to escape the French Revolution?

A. Sulpicians.

Q. What monument south of St. Mary's City is the nation's smallest national cemetery?

A. Tulip Disaster Monument.

Q. Which president personally campaigned against Millard Tydings in 1938?

A. Franklin D. Roosevelt.

Q. What Quaker converted to Catholicism and became the first pastor of St. Ann's Church in Baltimore in 1873?

A. William Bartlett.

Q. Who was the first African American to run for the U.S. Senate from Maryland?

A. William Ashbie Hawkins.

Q. Established in 1830, what is the oldest Jewish congregation in Maryland?

A. Baltimore Hebrew Congregation.

Q. Whose body was quietly removed from the arsenal of the Washington Navy yard and buried in Baltimore on June 6, 1869?

A. John Wilkes Booth.

Q. Which CIA director was buried in Green Mount Cemetery in 1969?

A. Allen Dulles.

Q. Who was Baltimore's first city councilman of Polish ancestry?

A. Edward I. Novak.

ARTS & LITERATURE

CHAPTER FOUR

Q. What humorist and author of *The Christmas That Almost Wasn't* lived in Maryland?

A. Ogden Nash.

Q. What is the name of America's first newspaper, published in Annapolis in 1727?

A. *Maryland Gazette*.

Q. Who is known as the "Sage of Baltimore"?

A. H. L. Mencken.

Q. What was the bestselling book by Maryland's Cardinal James Gibbons?

A. *The Faith of Our Fathers*.

Q. Baltimore's main public library, which contains a notable Maryland collection, was named for which merchant?

A. Enoch Pratt.

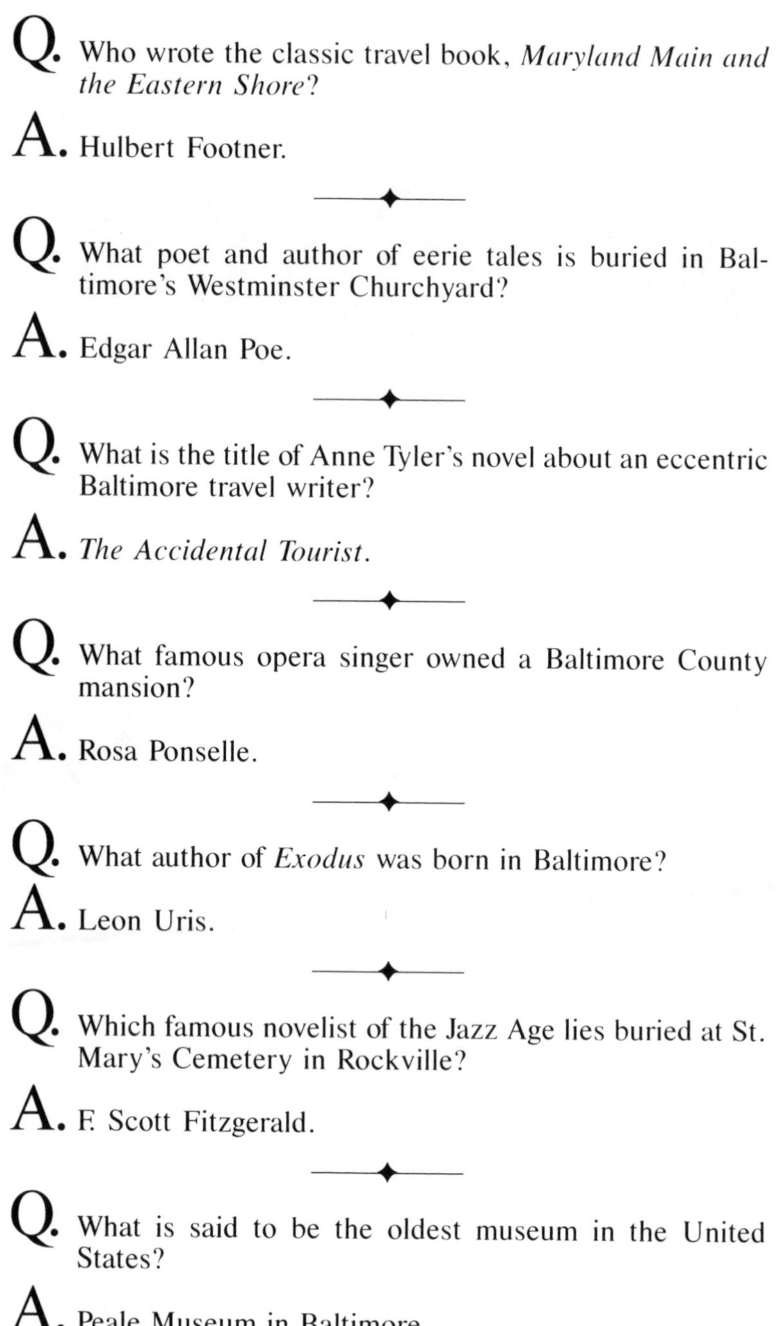

Q. Who wrote the classic travel book, *Maryland Main and the Eastern Shore*?

A. Hulbert Footner.

—◆—

Q. What poet and author of eerie tales is buried in Baltimore's Westminster Churchyard?

A. Edgar Allan Poe.

—◆—

Q. What is the title of Anne Tyler's novel about an eccentric Baltimore travel writer?

A. *The Accidental Tourist*.

—◆—

Q. What famous opera singer owned a Baltimore County mansion?

A. Rosa Ponselle.

—◆—

Q. What author of *Exodus* was born in Baltimore?

A. Leon Uris.

—◆—

Q. Which famous novelist of the Jazz Age lies buried at St. Mary's Cemetery in Rockville?

A. F. Scott Fitzgerald.

—◆—

Q. What is said to be the oldest museum in the United States?

A. Peale Museum in Baltimore.

Q. What author of *Look Homeward Angel* died in Baltimore on September 15, 1938?

A. Thomas Wolfe.

Q. Where is the Maryland Shakespeare Festival held every summer?

A. St. Mary's City.

Q. What is the official state song?

A. "Maryland, My Maryland."

Q. What author of *Double Indemnity* was born in Annapolis and went to college in Chestertown?

A. James M. Cain.

Q. Maryland private eye Arthur Halstead has to postpone his Christmas shopping to solve a murder in which novel by William Edward Hayes?

A. *Black Chronicle*.

Q. What prolific mystery writer and author of *Murder in Maryland* lived in Annapolis?

A. Leslie Ford.

Q. What plantation in Hollywood contains a Chinese Chippendale staircase?

A. Sotterley.

Q. What author of *Ship of Fools* lived in College Park late in her life?

A. Katherine Anne Porter.

Q. What architect of the U.S. Capitol also designed the Basilica of the Assumption in Baltimore?

A. Benjamin Latrobe.

Q. Thorne Smith, the author of *Topper*, was born in what city in 1892?

A. Annapolis.

Q. Which Maryland-born author of such books as *The Jungle* ran for governor of California in 1934?

A. Upton Sinclair.

Q. Who sculpted a statue honoring Edgar Allan Poe, which can be seen in Baltimore?

A. Moses Ezekiel.

Q. What artist, born in Queen Anne's County, was one of the most notable in early America?

A. Charles Wilson Peale.

Q. Where was novelist John Barth born?

A. Cambridge.

Q. What Georgia-born novelist moved to Baltimore, taught at Johns Hopkins, and played flute for the Peabody Orchestra?

A. Sidney Lanier.

Q. Which Maryland-born writer is known for *The Greatest Story Ever Told*?

A. Fulton Oursler.

Q. Mystery writer Dashiell Hammett, author of *The Thin Man*, had a job doing what in Baltimore?

A. Pinkerton detective.

Q. What classical scholar, author of *The Greek Way* and *The Roman Way*, was headmistress of the Bryn Mawr School in Baltimore for twenty-six years?

A. Edith Hamilton.

Q. Where is the Maryland Christmas Show, an arts-and-crafts-lovers delight, held just after Thanksgiving?

A. Frederick.

Q. What Baltimore-born publisher and bookseller founded the Paris bookshop, Shakespeare and Company?

A. Sylvia Beach.

Q. Which Baltimorean was America's first female journalist?

A. Anne Royall.

Q. Victor Kamkin owns a famous Russian-language book store in which Montgomery County town?

A. Rockville.

Q. What internationally acclaimed horn virtuoso established the Maryland Symphony?

A. Barry Tuckwell.

Q. Which Maryland-born slave wrote the book *Truth Stranger Than Fiction* that was the basis for Harriet Beecher Stowe's *Uncle Tom's Cabin*?

A. Josiah Henson, who escaped slavery by fleeing to Canada in 1830, where he beame a Methodist preacher and abolitionist.

Q. What Baltimore-born historian wrote the classic Titanic book, *A Night to Remember*?

A. Walter Lord.

Q. Where is the Walters Art Gallery?

A. Baltimore.

Q. For whom is Johns Hopkins University Library named?

A. Milton S. Eisenhower.

Q. What author of the classic murder mystery *The Bellamy Trial* was born in Silver Spring in 1890?

A. Frances Noyes Hart.

Q. Which town hosts the Maryland Symphony Orchestra?

A. Hagerstown.

Q. What Centreville publishing firm is noted for its books about Maryland?

A. Tidewater Publishers.

Q. Which Hyattsville resident wrote *The Postman Always Rings Twice*?

A. James M. Cain.

Q. What author of *A Private Place*, an important study of the Lizzie Borden murder case, died in Baltimore in 1981?

A. Victoria Lincoln.

Q. What is the motto of the *Baltimore Sun* newspaper?

A. Light for All.

Q. Which Maryland county pioneered bookmobile library services to remote country areas with a two-horse wagon filled with books?

A. Washington.

Q. What architect inaugurated the Gothic Revival in America with his design for the chapel at the Catholic seminary in Baltimore?

A. Maximilien Godefroy.

Q. What Baltimore-born poet wrote *Diving into the Wreck*?

A. Adrienne Rich.

⸻✦⸻

Q. Which Montgomery County town, which was near major Civil War battles and troop movements, boasts a nationally known Civil War bookstore?

A. Gaithersburg.

⸻✦⸻

Q. Leslie Ford's mystery novel, *By the Watchmen's Clock*, takes place at which Annapolis university?

A. St. Johns.

⸻✦⸻

Q. The Baltimore suspense novel *Razor Game* was written by what author of *Six Days of the Condor*?

A. James Grady.

⸻✦⸻

Q. Sidney Nyburg wrote which book about old Baltimore legends?

A. *Buried Rose*.

⸻✦⸻

Q. Which excellent Bethesda bookstore is called the "Home of Masterpiece Murder and Collectible Crime"?

A. The Mystery Bookshop.

⸻✦⸻

Q. Who was Maryland's first poet laureate?

A. Maria Briscoe Croker.

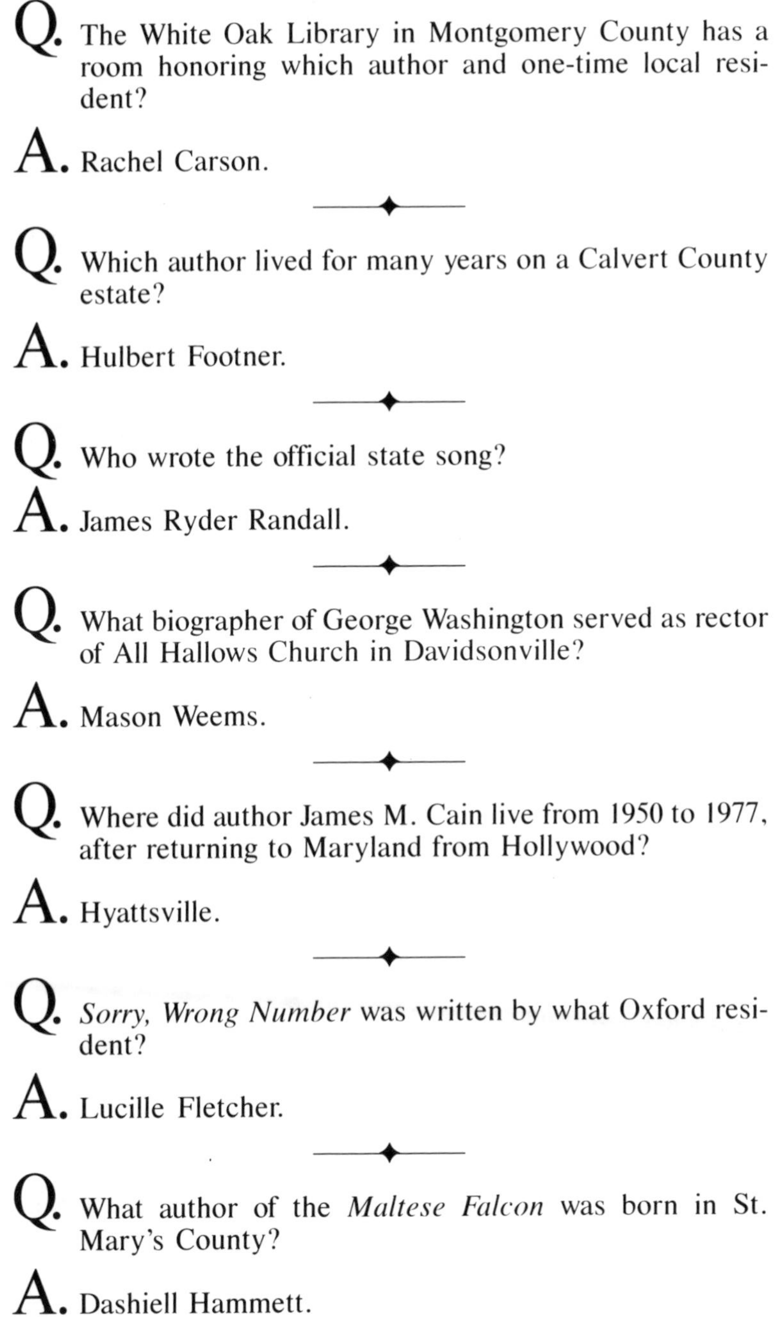

Q. The White Oak Library in Montgomery County has a room honoring which author and one-time local resident?

A. Rachel Carson.

Q. Which author lived for many years on a Calvert County estate?

A. Hulbert Footner.

Q. Who wrote the official state song?

A. James Ryder Randall.

Q. What biographer of George Washington served as rector of All Hallows Church in Davidsonville?

A. Mason Weems.

Q. Where did author James M. Cain live from 1950 to 1977, after returning to Maryland from Hollywood?

A. Hyattsville.

Q. *Sorry, Wrong Number* was written by what Oxford resident?

A. Lucille Fletcher.

Q. What author of the *Maltese Falcon* was born in St. Mary's County?

A. Dashiell Hammett.

Q. Who wrote *Rob of the Bowl*, which tells the story of early Maryland?

A. Thomas Pendleton Kennedy.

Q. Who wrote *Kennedy Square*, a popular 1911 novel about Baltimore?

A. F. Hopkinson Smith.

Q. What architect designed the Lovely Lane Methodist Church?

A. Stanford White.

Q. Which nineteenth century novelist wrote *Tales of the Chesapeake*, a collection of local-color stories?

A. George Alfred Townsend.

Q. Who is the author of *Richard Carvel*, an 1899 novel about colonial Maryland?

A. Winston Churchill.

Q. Which renowned novelist lived in Baltimore from 1932 to 1935?

A. F. Scott Fitzgerald.

Q. Which Don Tracy novel concerns the lynching of a black man in Maryland?

A. *How Sleeps the Beast.*

Q. Whose novel *Three Lives* is set in Baltimore?

A. Gertrude Stein.

Q. Where did novelist Hervey Allen study from 1909 to 1911?

A. U.S. Naval Academy.

Q. Which Baltimore native wrote *A Rebel War Clerk's Diary*?

A. John Beauchamp Jones.

Q. What Garrett Park author wrote the classic children's book *Ferdinand the Bull*?

A. Munro Leaf.

Q. What author of *On the Yard* died in a Baltimore traffic accident on April 7, 1980?

A. Malcolm Braly.

Q. The official state song uses the music of which German Christmas carol?

A. "O Tannenbaum."

Q. Which famous poet taught at St. Charles College for many years?

A. John Bannister Tabb.

Q. Martha Finley, author of the Elsie Dunsmore books, once lived in what town?

A. Elkton.

Q. Where was author and clergyman Mason Weems born?

A. Herring Bay.

Q. Which novel by George Townsend immortalized the exploits of notorious Marylander Patty Cannon?

A. *The Entailed Hat.*

Q. What author lived in a manor house called Bonfield in Oxford?

A. Hervey Allen.

Q. Where did H. L. Mencken deliver a lecture entitled "How to Catch a Husband" in the spring of 1923?

A. Goucher College in Towson.

Q. What was the name of the renowned Catholic publishing house founded by John Eckenrode and headquartered in Westminster?

A. Newman Press.

Q. Which lyric poet was born in the village of Waverly?

A. Lizette Reese.

Q. What noted biographer attended St. Timothy's school in Catonsville?

A. Catherine Drinker Bowen.

Q. What "poet-priest of the Confederacy" was born in Hagerstown?

A. Father Abram Ryan.

Q. What author of *U.S.A.* was living in Cross Keys Village when he died in 1970?

A. John Dos Passos.

Q. What is the oldest coeducational college south of the Mason-Dixon Line?

A. Western Maryland College.

Q. Which Baltimore firm published Edgar Allan Poe's *Tamerlane* in 1829?

A. Hatch and Dunning.

Q. Which Irish-Catholic publishing firm maintained its U.S. branch in Baltimore?

A. Helicon Press.

Q. What English Jesuit wrote the first book about Maryland in 1635?

A. Father Andrew White.

Q. Which Maryland author advised President Lincoln on Civil War military strategy?

A. Anna Ella Carroll.

Q. Which Anglican clergyman was the earliest advocate of a public library in Maryland?

A. Rev. Thomas Bray.

Q. What is Towson State University's collegiate newspaper called?

A. *Towerlight.*

Q. Which author, a long-time confirmed bachelor, married Sara Haardt in 1930?

A. H. L. Mencken.

Q. Whose novel *Bingo* is set in the fictional town of Runnymede, Maryland?

A. Rita Mae Brown.

Q. Which seventeenth-century author wrote *Character of the Province of Maryland*?

A. George Alsop.

Q. What highly praised 1942 novel by Harry Sylvester probes race relations in southern Maryland?

A. *Dearly Beloved.*

Q. What clergyman of the Baltimore Cathedral is considered the first Catholic novelist in America?

A. Charles Constantine Pise.

—✦—

Q. Which Frederick native wrote *History of Maryland*, which covers the years 1634 to 1848?

A. James McSherry.

—✦—

Q. Who wrote a fanciful, comic satire about a visit to Maryland called *The Sot-Weed Factor* in 1708?

A. Ebenezer Cook.

—✦—

Q. Which excellent secondhand bookshop has branches in Gaithersburg and Rockville?

A. Book Alcove.

—✦—

Q. Who wrote the highly praised novel about Chesapeake oyster men, called *The Lord's Oysters*, in 1957?

A. Gilbert Byron.

—✦—

Q. What is the sequel to *The Lord's Oysters* called?

A. *Done Crabbin*, published in 1990.

—✦—

Q. What author's home in Denton is now a bed and breakfast inn?

A. Sophie Kerr's.

Q. In what Maryland town does Dorothy Sucher's mystery *Dead Men Don't Marry* take place?

A. Bowie.

Q. Helen Corse Barney's Civil War novel, *Green Rose of Furley*, concerns the antislavery activities of which religious group?

A. Quakers.

Q. Who wrote *Giles Goat Boy* and *The End of the Road*?

A. John Barth.

Q. Which James M. Cain novel is about an ex-boxer in a southern Maryland town?

A. *Galatea*.

Q. Which Natalie Carlson novel takes place at the Visitation Academy in Frederick?

A. *Luvvy and the Girls*.

Q. Who wrote a suspense novel set on the Eastern Shore called *The Strange Blue Yawl*?

A. Lucille Fletcher.

Q. Murder takes place in a Baltimore antique store in which novel by Lucine Flynn?

A. *Antique and Deadly*.

Q. Who wrote the 1901 novel *The Tower of Wye*, which takes place on the Eastern Shore?

A. William Henry Babcock.

—✦—

Q. What national historic landmark designed by William Buckland is an outstanding example of American colonial architecture?

A. Hammond-Harwood House in Annapolis.

—✦—

Q. Who wrote *Cap'n Sue*, a tale of Chesapeake Bay bootleggers?

A. Hulbert Footner.

—✦—

Q. Who wrote *The Sound of Petticoats*, a collection of short stories about the people of the Eastern Shore?

A. Sophie Kerr.

—✦—

Q. Black magic and witchcraft in the Maryland hunt country occur in which Barbara Michaels novel?

A. *Prince of Darkness*.

—✦—

Q. Which 1902 novel by F. Hopkinson Smith is concerned with a Baltimore painter?

A. *The Fortunes of Oliver Horn*.

—✦—

Q. Where does prolific author Barbara Mertz live?

A. Frederick.

Q. What is the state's largest newspaper in circulation?

A. *Baltimore Sun.*

Q. Who wrote the historical novel *Crimson Is the Eastern Shore*?

A. Don Tracy.

Q. Augusta Tucker's novels, *Miss Susie Slagle's* and *The Man Miss Susie Loved*, are about students at which Maryland university?

A. Johns Hopkins.

Q. What author lived at 203 North Amity Street in Baltimore?

A. Edgar Allan Poe.

Q. What author of the poem "The Marshes of Glynn" lies buried in Baltimore's Green Mount Cemetery?

A. Sidney Lanier.

Q. What Pat McGerr novel takes place at the Olney Theatre?

A. *Murder Is Absurd.*

Q. Who is the fictional Eastern Shore crab that appears in a delightful series of children's books by Priscilla Cummings?

A. Chadwick.

Q. What is the name of the Maryland Library Association's journal?

A. *The Crab.*

—◆—

Q. Which Prince George's County library branch has a notable collection of books about African Americans?

A. Oxon Hill Branch Library.

—◆—

Q. What mystery writer and one-time professor at Montgomery College won the Nero Wolfe Award in 1983?

A. Martha Grimes.

—◆—

Q. Which best-selling Maryland author wrote *Red Storm Rising* and *The Hunt for Red October*?

A. Tom Clancy.

—◆—

Q. What Bethesda resident wrote *The Politics of Rich and Poor*?

A. Kevin Phillips.

—◆—

Q. Which professor at the University of Maryland wrote *Breaking Bread* and *White Water*?

A. Joyce Kornblatt.

—◆—

Q. What unique bookshop is on Cordell Avenue in Bethesda?

A. Travel Books Unlimited.

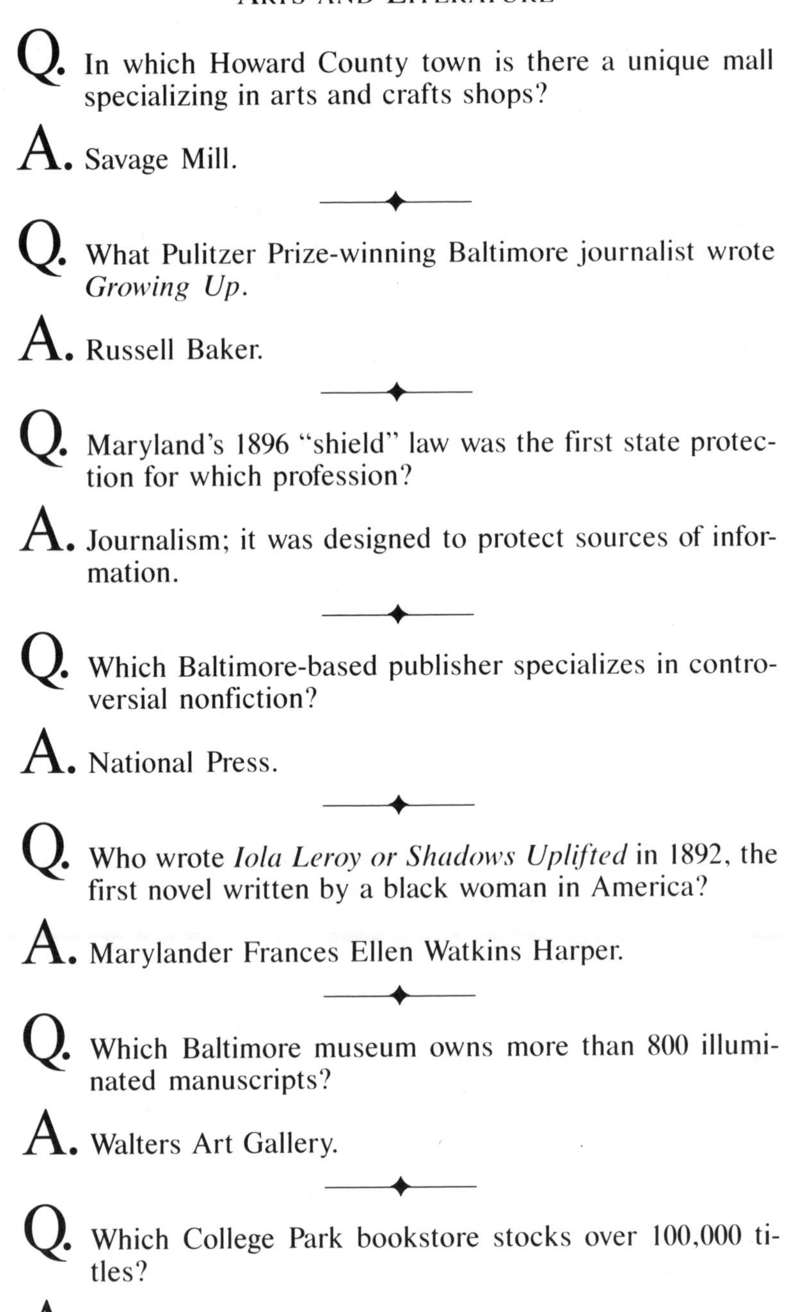

Q. In which Howard County town is there a unique mall specializing in arts and crafts shops?

A. Savage Mill.

—◆—

Q. What Pulitzer Prize-winning Baltimore journalist wrote *Growing Up*.

A. Russell Baker.

—◆—

Q. Maryland's 1896 "shield" law was the first state protection for which profession?

A. Journalism; it was designed to protect sources of information.

—◆—

Q. Which Baltimore-based publisher specializes in controversial nonfiction?

A. National Press.

—◆—

Q. Who wrote *Iola Leroy or Shadows Uplifted* in 1892, the first novel written by a black woman in America?

A. Marylander Frances Ellen Watkins Harper.

—◆—

Q. Which Baltimore museum owns more than 800 illuminated manuscripts?

A. Walters Art Gallery.

—◆—

Q. Which College Park bookstore stocks over 100,000 titles?

A. Maryland Book Exchange.

Q. What is the oldest music school in the United States?

A. Peabody Conservatory in Baltimore.

Q. Baltimore's new Hackerman House museum specializes in what type of art?

A. Asian.

Q. What is the name of Douglas Hank's novel about a group of Maryland watermen who build a racing yacht to recapture the America's Cup for the United States?

A. *Muskrat.*

Q. Where did Michael Chabon, author of *Mysteries of Pittsburgh*, live during his youth?

A. Columbia.

Q. What book about the Chesapeake Bay by William Warner won the Pulitzer Prize in 1977?

A. *Beautiful Swimmers.*

Q. What prominent Chesapeake Bay artist is known for his lithographs of skipjacks and lighthouses?

A. John Moll.

Q. What is Maryland's only feminist bookstore?

A. The 31st Street Bookshop.

Q. The prestigious old Newspaper Guild is headquartered in which town close to Washington, D.C.?

A. Silver Spring.

—◆—

Q. Which Montgomery County town is home to the Music Critics Association?

A. Rockville.

—◆—

Q. Which 1989 novel by Bob Cairns takes place among Maryland minor league baseball players?

A. *The Comeback Kids*.

—◆—

Q. What author of the 1954 Edgar-winning mystery novel *The Perfectionist* died in Glen Arm in 1988?

A. Lane Kauffman.

—◆—

Q. Which Montgomery County town has a high school named for Walt Whitman?

A. Bethesda.

—◆—

Q. Which controversial columnist owned a mansion at 13130 River Road in Potomac?

A. Drew Pearson.

—◆—

Q. Preston Pairo's 1991 mystery novel *Beach Money* takes place in which town?

A. Ocean City.

Q. How many colleges and universities, including two-year institutions, does Maryland have?

A. Fifty-seven.

Q. What author lived at 1524 Hollins Street in Baltimore most of his life?

A. H. L. Mencken.

Q. Which Maryland painter is a noted watercolorist who conducts several workshops each year?

A. James Drake Iams.

Q. What son of a Maryland oysterman founded the first publishing house after the Civil War in 1866?

A. Henry Holt.

Q. Which black educator and author lived at 2302 Montebello Terrace in Baltimore during the 1940s?

A. W. E. B. DuBois.

Q. What used and rare bookshop in Frederick stocks over 300,000 volumes?

A. Wonder Book and Video.

Q. What Baltimore-born opera star left her entire art collection to the Baltimore Museum of Art on her death in 1963?

A. Mabel Garrison.

Q. When did the *Maryland Historical Magazine* begin publication?

A. 1906.

Q. Which historian of Maryland also wrote several mysteries set in the state?

A. Frederic Kummer.

Q. Who wrote the social history, *The Amiable Baltimoreans*?

A. Francis Beirne.

Q. What renowned photographer of Maryland and the Chesapeake region was buried at Green Mount Cemetery in 1970?

A. Aubrey Bodine.

Q. On which poet's Baltimore grave is the epitaph, "I am lit with the sun"?

A. Sidney Lanier.

Q. What is the official newspaper of the Catholic Archdiocese of Baltimore?

A. *Catholic Review*.

Q. Which P. M. Carlson mystery is set in suburban Maryland?

A. *Bad Blood*.

Q. Where is the Square Corner Bookshop?

A. Frederick.

Q. Which town has a newspaper called the *Maryland Gazette*?

A. Glen Burnie.

Q. Dorothy Parker, known for her light, satirical verse, has her ashes buried where in Baltimore?

A. NAACP headquarters.

Q. What Confederate veteran wrote a highly praised history of Baltimore?

A. J. Thomas Scharf.

Q. Which Elkton newspaper, founded in 1841, still retains the name of a now defunct political party?

A. *Cecil Whig*.

Q. What author of the first history of American Methodism is buried in Baltimore?

A. Jessie Lee.

Q. Which monthly travel magazine is published in Greenbelt?

A. *Mid-Atlantic Country*.

Q. Which Maryland county library circulates more books per capita than any other major library system in the United States?

A. Baltimore.

Q. What is the name of the University of Maryland campus newspaper?

A. *Diamondback*.

Q. Which country music biographer was born in Leonardtown?

A. Don Cusic.

Q. What museum, housed in a private home in Monktown, contains an exceptional collection of Thai and Southeast Asian arts?

A. Breezewood Foundation.

Q. Over whose Baltimore grave was a monument erected on November 17, 1875?

A. Edgar Allan Poe.

Q. Which Jesuit college in Baltimore was founded in 1852?

A. Loyola.

Q. What 1984 book of watercolors by James Drake Iams has become a regional classic?

A. *Bayside Impressions*.

Q. Where does Maryland rank in the number of Georgetown University alumni?

A. First.

Q. What percentage of Maryland residents who are college freshmen attend college in Maryland?

A. 75 percent.

Q. Whose column, "Oysterback Tales," is a popular feature in the *Baltimore Sun*?

A. Helen Chappell.

Q. Which novelist lived on Chateau Avenue and on Canterbury Road in Baltimore?

A. John Dos Passos.

Q. Which modern novelist used the title of Ebenezer Cook's *The Sot-Weed Factor* for his popular 1960 book?

A. John Barth.

Q. What unique architectural structure is represented by Cardinal Edward Mooney's boyhood home in Mount Savage?

A. "Company houses" built by one of the mining companies.

Q. What art school is located in Silver Spring?

A. Maryland College of Art and Design.

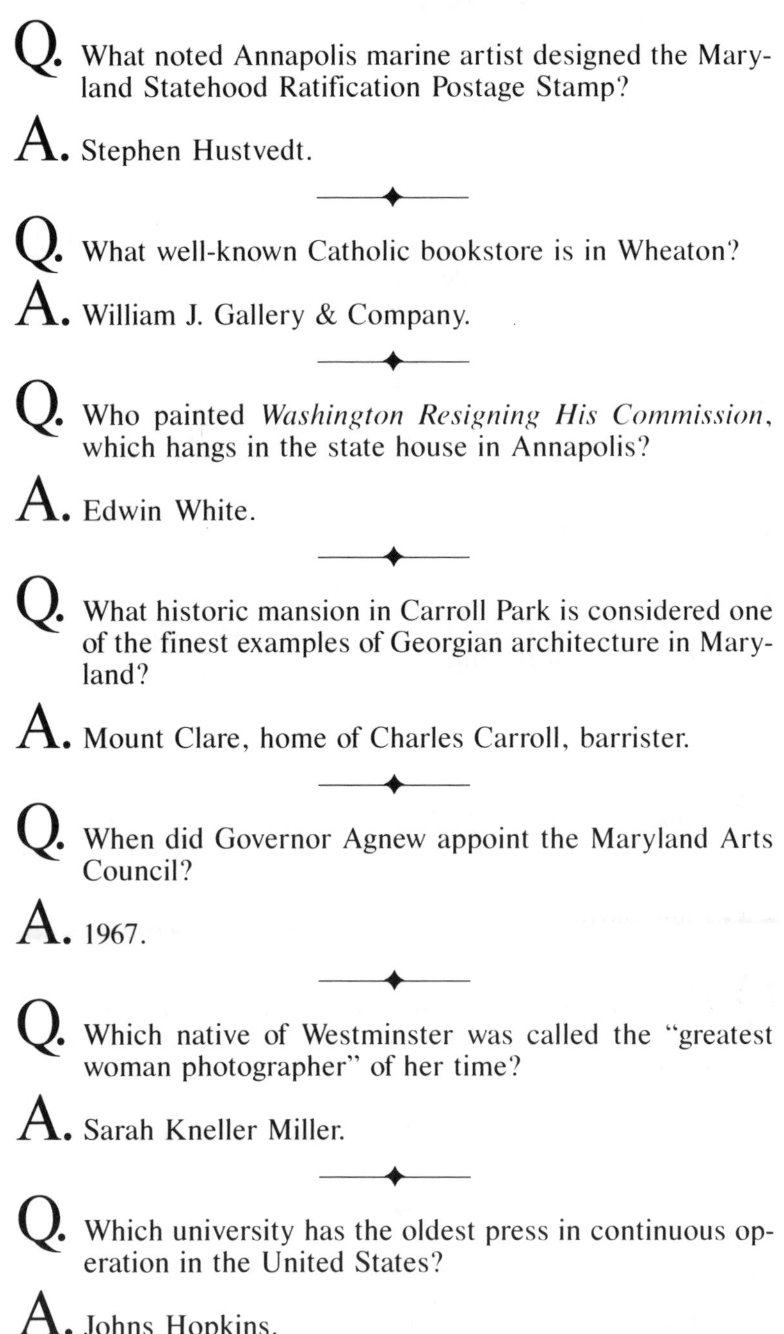

Q. What noted Annapolis marine artist designed the Maryland Statehood Ratification Postage Stamp?

A. Stephen Hustvedt.

Q. What well-known Catholic bookstore is in Wheaton?

A. William J. Gallery & Company.

Q. Who painted *Washington Resigning His Commission*, which hangs in the state house in Annapolis?

A. Edwin White.

Q. What historic mansion in Carroll Park is considered one of the finest examples of Georgian architecture in Maryland?

A. Mount Clare, home of Charles Carroll, barrister.

Q. When did Governor Agnew appoint the Maryland Arts Council?

A. 1967.

Q. Which native of Westminster was called the "greatest woman photographer" of her time?

A. Sarah Kneller Miller.

Q. Which university has the oldest press in continuous operation in the United States?

A. Johns Hopkins.

Q. Which James Michener novel takes place in Maryland?

A. *Chesapeake.*

Q. Who was America's first black portrait painter?

A. Baltimore resident Joshua Johnston.

Q. The University of Maryland library maintains a room honoring the memory of which author who lived in College Park?

A. Katherine Anne Porter.

Q. What is the subject of Jane Wilson's 1991 book, *The Very Quiet Baltimoreans*?

A. Cemeteries.

Q. What author, a resident of Sion Hill in Harford County, won the Newbery Medal for her children's biography of Louisa May Alcott?

A. Cornelia Lynde Meigs.

Q. Which 1991 mystery novel by Mary Cahill takes place in suburban Maryland?

A. *Carpool.*

Q. Maryland novelist Barbara Mertz endowed a $100,000 scholarship fund to encourage minority students interested in writing mysteries at what college?

A. Hood College in Frederick.

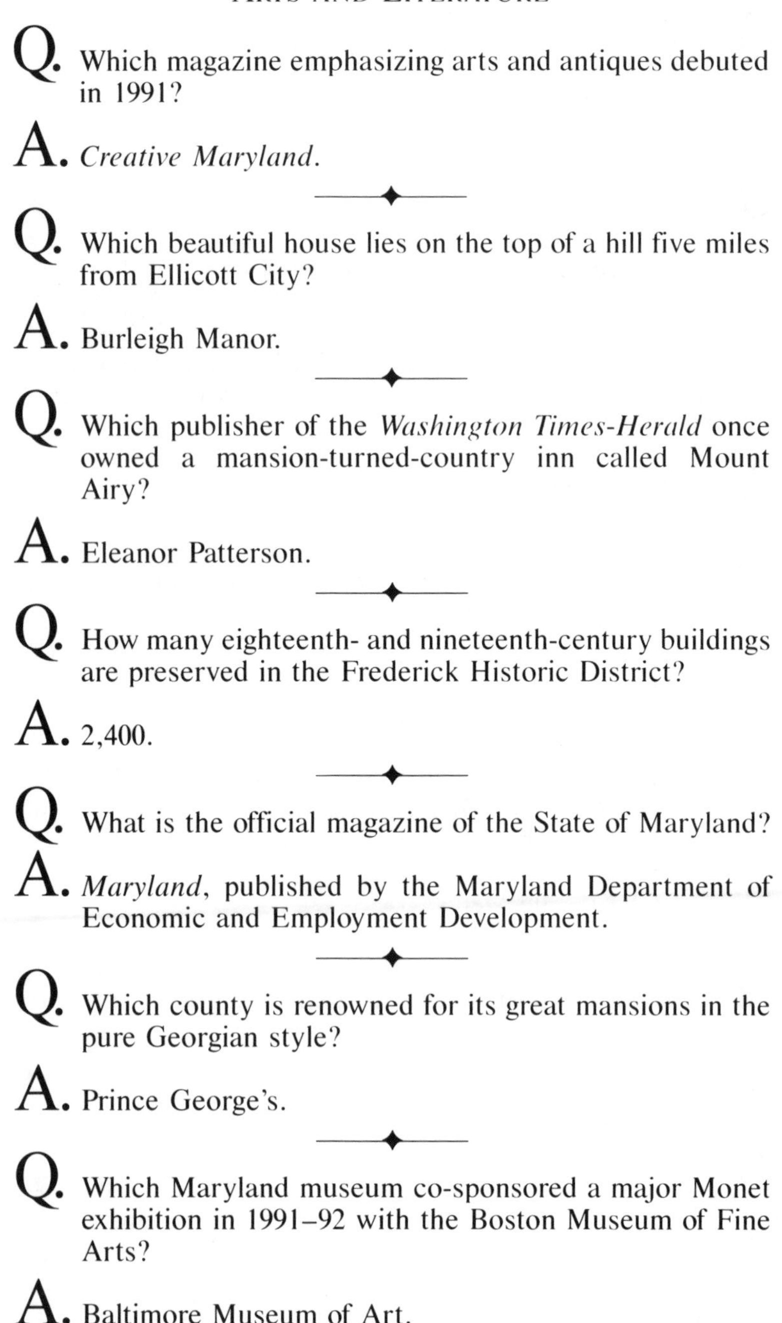

Q. Which magazine emphasizing arts and antiques debuted in 1991?

A. *Creative Maryland.*

Q. Which beautiful house lies on the top of a hill five miles from Ellicott City?

A. Burleigh Manor.

Q. Which publisher of the *Washington Times-Herald* once owned a mansion-turned-country inn called Mount Airy?

A. Eleanor Patterson.

Q. How many eighteenth- and nineteenth-century buildings are preserved in the Frederick Historic District?

A. 2,400.

Q. What is the official magazine of the State of Maryland?

A. *Maryland*, published by the Maryland Department of Economic and Employment Development.

Q. Which county is renowned for its great mansions in the pure Georgian style?

A. Prince George's.

Q. Which Maryland museum co-sponsored a major Monet exhibition in 1991–92 with the Boston Museum of Fine Arts?

A. Baltimore Museum of Art.

SPORTS & LEISURE

CHAPTER FIVE

Q. What is the state sport?

A. Jousting.

Q. What was Maryland's only professional football team?

A. Baltimore Colts.

Q. Jim Palmer played what position for the Baltimore Orioles?

A. Pitcher.

Q. Maryland is noted for what famous resort town?

A. Ocean City.

Q. What is the name of the once-popular amusement park near Washington, D.C.?

A. Glen Echo Park.

Q. What is Maryland's only major league baseball team?

A. Baltimore Orioles.

Q. In what league does the University of Maryland play football?

A. Atlantic Coast Conference.

Q. Where do the Georgetown Hoyas play their home basketball games?

A. Capital Centre in Landover.

Q. The birthplace of what New York Yankee slugger is now a museum in Baltimore?

A. Babe Ruth.

Q. In what Maryland county do baseball fans root for the Philadelphia Phillies instead of the Orioles?

A. Cecil.

Q. The Maryland Bays compete in which sport?

A. Soccer.

Q. In what year did the Baltimore Colts win their only Super Bowl?

A. 1971.

Q. What is the name of Baltimore's famous racetrack?

A. Pimlico.

Q. Who was named the Most Valuable Player in the 1970 World Series?

A. Orioles third baseman Brooks Robinson.

Q. What is the popular sport in the elegant town of Potomac?

A. Polo.

Q. When did the Baltimore Colts move to Indianapolis?

A. March 1984.

Q. During Prohibition, Baltimoreans who wanted beer with their seafood looked for what sign displayed on a restaurant?

A. Red Hard Crab.

Q. What Baltimore resident was called the "Babe Ruth of badminton"?

A. Judy Devlin Hashman.

Q. Which vice president pitched the first ball at the Orioles' first American League game in 1954?

A. Richard Nixon.

Q. Where is the Maryland State Fair held each summer?

A. Timonium.

Q. What sport is associated with the town of Laurel?

A. Horse racing.

Q. Caught by Cecil Brown in Ocean City, how much did the IGFA (International Game Fish Association) All-Tackle World Record Atlantic bigeye tuna weigh?

A. 375 pounds, 8 ounces (record as of September 1, 1990).

Q. In what year did the Orioles suffer a twenty-one-game losing streak at the beginning of the season?

A. 1988.

Q. What Maryland-born football player won the Heisman Trophy while playing for Boston College in 1984?

A. Doug Flutie.

Q. What Pimlico-based organization is the oldest sporting association in the United States?

A. Maryland Jockey Club.

Q. In what year did the University of Maryland win the national championship in college football?

A. 1953.

Q. Who won the Women's Highpower Rifle category at the 1987 National Outdoor Rifle and Pistol Championships?

A. Kathy M. Livingstone of Fallston.

Q. In 1974, what famed publisher was the first person to pilot a hot-air balloon coast to coast over the United States, starting in Oregon and landing in Maryland?

A. Malcolm Forbes.

Q. When did Hank Bauer become Oriole manager?

A. 1964.

Q. What is the nickname of the University of Maryland football team?

A. Terrapins or Terps.

Q. Which Oriole first baseman won the Golden Glove Award in 1982, 1983, and 1984?

A. Eddie Murray.

Q. Who was the first black member of the Baseball Writers Association of America?

A. Sam Lacy, sports editor for the Baltimore *Afro American*.

Q. What steeplechase race has been held at Worthington Farms in Glyndon since 1894?

A. Maryland Hunt Cup.

Q. Randy White, defensive tackle for Maryland, won what three awards for best lineman in 1974?

A. Rockne, Lombardi, and Outland trophies.

—◆—

Q. What was the name of Maryland's first covered mall, which opened in 1958?

A. Harundale.

—◆—

Q. What event is held at Christ Church in Port Republic each year on the last Saturday in August?

A. A jousting tournament.

—◆—

Q. Which native of Takoma Park served as baseball commissioner from 1969 to 1984?

A. Bowie Kuhn.

—◆—

Q. Who is the diminutive NBA basketball player who was born in Baltimore in 1965 and is nicknamed "Mugsy"?

A. Tyrone Bogues.

—◆—

Q. In what month is the Preakness horse race held at Pimlico?

A. May.

—◆—

Q. What sport is commemorated in a Hall of Fame in the athletic building at Johns Hopkins University?

A. Lacrosse.

Q. What welterweight boxing champion lives in Potomac?

A. Sugar Ray Leonard.

Q. Who lost to the Orioles in the 1983 World Series?

A. Philadelphia Phillies.

Q. What prize is given to the winner of the Preakness Stakes at Pimlico?

A. Woodlawn Cup.

Q. What gambling activity was legalized in 1947 in southern Maryland?

A. Slot machines.

Q. What clipper ship, which sank in 1986, visited ports around the world to promote the state of Maryland?

A. *Pride of Baltimore*.

Q. Who was the major league baseball star who was born in Sudlersville in Queen Anne's County on October 22, 1907?

A. James Emory ("Jimmie") Foxx.

Q. What Maryland-born tennis player won the Wimbledon women's doubles match from 1981 to 1984 and again in 1986?

A. Pam Shriver, with Martina Navratilova.

Q. In what year did Maryland beat Tennessee 28-13 in the Sugar Bowl?

A. 1952.

Q. What sport was nearly outlawed by the Maryland General Assembly in 1920?

A. Horse racing.

Q. Who was the Most Valuable Player in the 1966 World Series?

A. Frank Robinson.

Q. Who was Maryland's college football Coach of the Year in 1953?

A. Jim Tatum.

Q. What was Oriole player Brooks Robinson's now-retired number?

A. 5.

Q. Who was the coach that led the Navy lacrosse team to eight consecutive national championships, 1959 to 1966.

A. Willis Peter Bilderback.

Q. Who coached the Colts to their 1971 Super Bowl victory?

A. Don McCafferty.

Q. What is the state's largest freshwater lake?

A. Deep Creek Lake near McHenry in Garrett County.

Q. What baseball great was born at 216 Emory Street in Baltimore?

A. Babe Ruth.

Q. Which Baltimorean was a star outfielder for the Detroit Tigers from 1953 to 1974 and the youngest player to win the batting title?

A. Al Kaline.

Q. What horseracing magazine has been published in Baltimore since 1924?

A. *Turf and Sport Digest*.

Q. Who was the only Oriole to be a triple crown winner?

A. Frank Robinson in 1966.

Q. Since 1895, how many times has the Navy rowing team won the Intercollegiate Rowing Association Regatta?

A. Twelve, second only to Cornell as of 1990.

Q. Who defeated the Colts in the 1969 Super Bowl?

A. New York Jets.

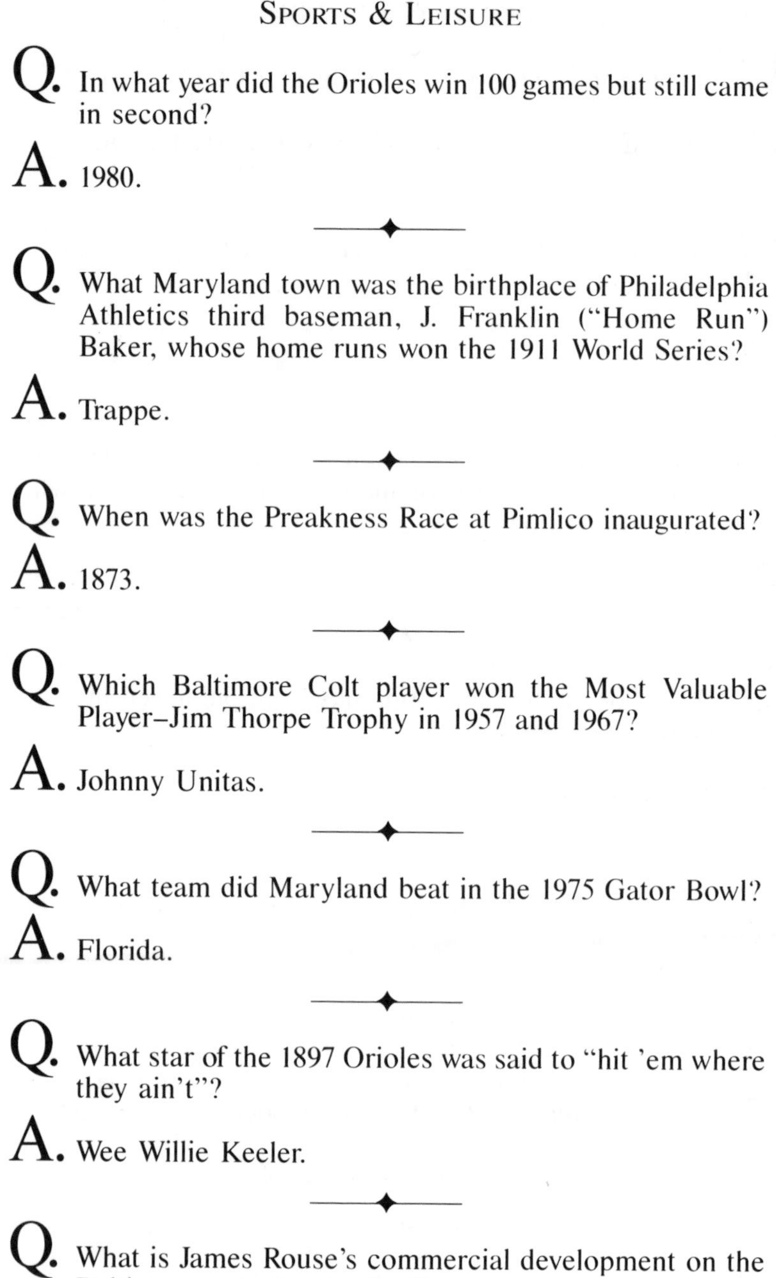

Q. In what year did the Orioles win 100 games but still came in second?

A. 1980.

Q. What Maryland town was the birthplace of Philadelphia Athletics third baseman, J. Franklin ("Home Run") Baker, whose home runs won the 1911 World Series?

A. Trappe.

Q. When was the Preakness Race at Pimlico inaugurated?

A. 1873.

Q. Which Baltimore Colt player won the Most Valuable Player–Jim Thorpe Trophy in 1957 and 1967?

A. Johnny Unitas.

Q. What team did Maryland beat in the 1975 Gator Bowl?

A. Florida.

Q. What star of the 1897 Orioles was said to "hit 'em where they ain't"?

A. Wee Willie Keeler.

Q. What is James Rouse's commercial development on the Baltimore waterfront called?

A. Harborplace.

Q. What is the name of the University of Maryland's basketball stadium?

A. Cole Field House.

⸻✦⸻

Q. Who was the Oriole outfielder who caught the series-ending fly ball to win the World Series in 1966?

A. Paul Blair.

⸻✦⸻

Q. As of 1990, which Thoroughbred recorded the best time at the Preakness?

A. Tank's Prospect in 1985.

⸻✦⸻

Q. What Baltimore-born running back for the Dallas Cowboys was named Rookie of the Year in 1969?

A. Calvin Hill.

⸻✦⸻

Q. What kind of competition is held every Labor Day on Deal Island?

A. Skipjack (fishing boat) Races.

⸻✦⸻

Q. What was the nickname of Colt star Lamar Davis?

A. "Racehorse."

⸻✦⸻

Q. What is Garrett County's ski resort called?

A. Wisp.

Q. The town of Hollywood hosts a Strawberry Festival each spring at which historic mansion?

A. Sotterly.

Q. Who managed the Orioles during their first World Series victory?

A. Hank Bauer.

Q. What is the name of the University of Maryland football arena?

A. Byrd Stadium.

Q. What is the nickname of the Hagerstown minor league baseball team?

A. Suns.

Q. Which defensive halfback returned as head coach of the Colts in 1963?

A. Don Shula.

Q. In what sport have the Johns Hopkins University Stickmen won nearly thirty championships?

A. Lacrosse.

Q. What team beat Maryland in the 1983 Citrus Bowl?

A. Tennessee.

Q. Which Oriole first baseman was named the Most Valuable Player in the 1970 League Championship Series?

A. Boog Powell.

Q. Who was the czar of Baltimore baseball from 1907 to 1928, a manager who won seven championships in the International League?

A. Jack Dunn.

Q. Who was named baseball's American League Manager of the Year in 1989?

A. Frank Robinson.

Q. Who beat the Colts in the 1964 NFL playoff?

A. Cleveland Browns.

Q. The Keys are the baseball minor league team in which town?

A. Frederick.

Q. Which Prince George's County facility is the largest shooting center on the East Coast?

A. Winchester Shooting Center.

Q. What is the name of Baltimore's lacrosse team?

A. The Thunder.

Q. The new Memorial Stadium is in what Baltimore neighborhood?

A. Camden Yards.

Q. Which Oriole pitcher struck out seven consecutive batters in his first major league appearance in 1978?

A. Sammy Stewart.

Q. At what Bethesda country club did President Eisenhower frequently play golf?

A. Burning Tree.

Q. Whom did the Colts play at their last home game in Baltimore on December 18, 1983?

A. Houston Oilers.

Q. Which Lonaconing native became a great pitcher and was elected to the Hall of Fame in 1947?

A. Lefty Grove.

Q. Who was the only Oriole in the 1990 All-Star game?

A. Cal Ripken, Jr.

Q. Which Prince George's County library has a noted collection of books on horse racing?

A. Bowie Regional.

Q. In which bowl did Maryland lose to Oklahoma 7-0 in 1954?

A. Orange.

Q. What caused Baltimore to close its schools and give city employees the afternoon off on April 15, 1954?

A. It was the first Baltimore Orioles baseball game after the franchise was moved from St. Louis.

Q. Where do the Frederick Keys play minor league baseball?

A. Grove Stadium.

Q. What Baltimore soccer team member was the 1984 Indoor Soccer League Playoff Most Valuable Player?

A. Scott Manning.

Q. What golf tournament is held at Avenel in Potomac every May?

A. Kemper Open.

Q. When did the Orioles first win a World Series?

A. 1966.

Q. How many Baltimore Colts have been elected to the Professional Football Hall of Fame?

A. Six.

Q. For whom was the Naval Academy's football stadium named?

A. Gov. Albert Ritchie.

Q. Which Washington Senators pitcher, nicknamed the "Big Train," owned a farm in Germantown, where he lived after retiring from the big leagues?

A. Walter Johnson.

Q. Who became the Orioles' manager on May 23, 1991?

A. John Oates.

Q. What offensive tackle, who played with the Colts from 1958 to 1959, is credited with giving Joe Namath the nickname "Broadway Joe"?

A. Sherman Plunkett.

Q. What beautiful animal is honored with a museum in the village of Barnesville?

A. Arabian horse.

Q. What sport is played when the Baltimore Blast gather?

A. Soccer.

Q. The Orioles beat which team in the 1970 World Series?

A. Cincinnati Reds.

Q. In which two years in a row were the Colts NFL champions?

A. 1958 and 1959.

—♦—

Q. Which town is known as the White Marlin Capital of the World?

A. Ocean City.

—♦—

Q. Where was Oriole star Cal Ripken, Jr., born?

A. Havre de Grace.

—♦—

Q. What "Cheers" scriptwriter did the radio play-by-play with regular Jon Miller for the Orioles 1991 season?

A. Ken Levine.

—♦—

Q. Where is the Cecil County Dragway, a popular place for stock car races?

A. North East.

—♦—

Q. Which Maryland player won both the Outland Trophy and the Rockne Award for best lineman in 1952?

A. Dick Modzelewski.

—♦—

Q. Who was manager of the 1983 World Champion Orioles?

A. Joe Altobelli.

Q. Which Oriole pitcher and Hall of Famer is also noted for his men's underwear ads?

A. Jim Palmer.

Q. Steeplechase races are held at Fair Hill in which town?

A. Elkton.

Q. In what game did Maryland beat Tennessee 28-27 in 1984?

A. Sun Bowl, now called the John Hancock Bowl.

Q. In 1954, the first year the Baltimore Orioles played in the American League, what did bleacher seats cost on opening day?

A. 75 cents.

Q. Brooklyn Dodger executive Branch Rickey owned a large farm near what Maryland town?

A. Chestertown.

Q. Who threw out the first ball at the 1991 opening day at Memorial Stadium?

A. Vice President Dan Quayle.

Q. What dam on the Susquehanna River forms a freshwater lake fourteen miles long?

A. Conowingo.

Q. How many games did the Orioles win in 1969 regular season play?

A. 109.

⸻◆⸻

Q. Which Detroit Tiger star graduated from Baltimore's Southern High School?

A. Al Kaline.

⸻◆⸻

Q. The Maryland lacrosse team has been in the Division I playoffs six times and won twice against what two teams?

A. Johns Hopkins (1973) and Navy (1975).

⸻◆⸻

Q. Who was the first Oriole to win a Gold Glove Award?

A. Brooks Robinson, in 1960.

⸻◆⸻

Q. Which magazine for English saddle riding enthusiasts is published in Gaithersburg?

A. *Horseplay*.

⸻◆⸻

Q. When did the Colts play their first season?

A. 1947.

⸻◆⸻

Q. On what day did Oriole Jim Palmer pitch his only no-hitter?

A. August 13, 1969.

Q. What sport do the Baltimore Skipjacks play?

A. Hockey.

Q. What Oriole lefthander won the Cy Young Award in 1979?

A. Mike Flanagan.

Q. Prior to 1954, when was the last major league baseball game played in Baltimore?

A. September 29, 1902.

Q. What was the name of Robert Goodman's musical score composed during the frenzied baseball summer of 1964?

A. "Pennant Fever."

Q. Where did boxing star Sugar Ray Leonard buy a six-bedroom mansion in the 1980s?

A. Potomac.

Q. What was the Colt star Alan Ameche's nickname?

A. "The Horse."

Q. What was the attendance on the Orioles' opening day in 1954?

A. 46,354.

Q. Who managed the Orioles during their first season?

A. Jimmy Dykes.

Q. Joseph Gans, who is buried in Baltimore, held what sports distinction?

A. He was the first black lightweight boxing champion of the world.

Q. What was Colts star Johnny Unitas's background, which made him a special hero to the residents of East Baltimore?

A. Lithuanian.

Q. Who was president of Pimlico Race Course from 1952 to 1986?

A. Herman Cohen.

Q. Who coached the Maryland football team in 1945?

A. Bear Bryant.

Q. In which World Series was Oriole Rick Dempsey named the Most Valuable Player?

A. 1983.

Q. How many years did Brooks Robinson play for the Orioles?

A. Twenty-three.

Q. What sporting event, held in August, begins in Annapolis and ends at St. Mary's College?

A. Governor's Cup Yacht Race.

Q. Where does Oriole Cal Ripkin, Jr., own a twenty-four-acre home?

A. Reistertown.

Q. Which two college football teams drew huge crowds when they faced off in Baltimore during the 1930s and 1940s?

A. Navy and Notre Dame.

Q. What team beat the Orioles in seven games in both the 1971 and 1979 World Series?

A. Pittsburgh Pirates.

Q. What was the name given to a baseball hit so hard that the runner made it to first base while the ball was still in the air?

A. "Baltimore chop."

Q. What river was the site of the 1989 Whitewater World Championship Races?

A. Savage.

Q. Whom did the Colts play in their first game?

A. Brooklyn Dodgers of the All America Conference.

Q. The New York Mets beat the Orioles in which World Series?

A. 1969.

Q. What is Ocean City's annual September celebration called?

A. Sunfest.

Q. Which Oriole player pitched a no-hitter against the Yankees in 1958?

A. Hoyt Wilhelm.

Q. What two college football teams played to a crowd of eighty thousand, including President and Mrs. Coolidge, in Baltimore's Municipal Stadium in 1924?

A. Army and Navy.

Q. What Baltimore disc jockey stayed on the air nonstop until the Orioles broke their 1988 losing streak?

A. Bob Rivers.

Q. What minor league baseball Class D league was based in Maryland?

A. Eastern Shore League.

Q. Which Oriole shortstop was named Rookie of the Year in 1960?

A. Ron Hansen.

Q. Which great New York Giants manager is buried at New Cathedral Cemetery in Baltimore?

A. John J. McGraw.

Q. When did the Orioles last win the World Series?

A. 1983.

Q. Where does Washington Bullets forward Bernard King own a fifty-six-acre home?

A. Brandywine.

Q. What team defeated the Baltimore Blast in the Major Indoor Soccer League (MISL) playoffs for the 1989–90 season?

A. San Diego.

Q. Which president attended the seventh game of the 1979 World Series in Baltimore?

A. Jimmy Carter.

Q. Which Baltimore native won twenty-seven games as a pitcher for the Philadelphia Athletics?

A. Eddie Rommel.

Q. In what year did the Orioles first draw two million fans to Memorial Stadium?

A. 1983.

Q. What soccer player from Maryland was on the 1990 World Cup National Team?

A. Desmond Armstrong, defender.

Q. What renowned attorney bought the Orioles on November 1, 1979?

A. Edward Bennett Williams.

Q. Which black league franchise boasted a million-dollar infield in the 1920s?

A. Baltimore Black Sox.

Q. Where did President Ronald Reagan sit during the 1984 opening game?

A. In the Orioles dugout.

Q. In what bowl did Maryland lose to Florida 35-20 in 1980?

A. Citrus.

Q. What Navy halfback won the Walter Camp Award for best back in 1960?

A. Joe Bellino.

Q. What Oriole fan became something of a folk hero, called the Squire of Section 34?

A. Wild Bill Hagy.

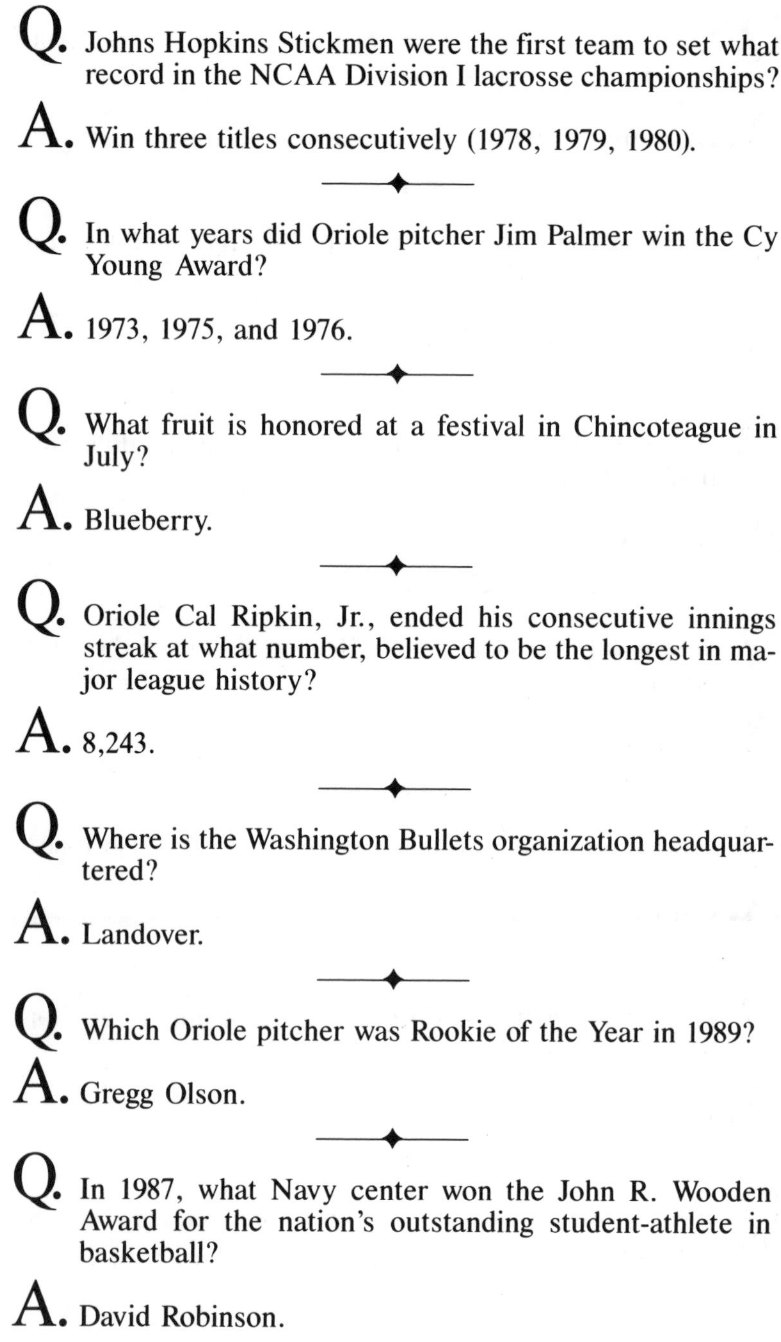

Q. Johns Hopkins Stickmen were the first team to set what record in the NCAA Division I lacrosse championships?

A. Win three titles consecutively (1978, 1979, 1980).

◆

Q. In what years did Oriole pitcher Jim Palmer win the Cy Young Award?

A. 1973, 1975, and 1976.

◆

Q. What fruit is honored at a festival in Chincoteague in July?

A. Blueberry.

◆

Q. Oriole Cal Ripkin, Jr., ended his consecutive innings streak at what number, believed to be the longest in major league history?

A. 8,243.

◆

Q. Where is the Washington Bullets organization headquartered?

A. Landover.

◆

Q. Which Oriole pitcher was Rookie of the Year in 1989?

A. Gregg Olson.

◆

Q. In 1987, what Navy center won the John R. Wooden Award for the nation's outstanding student-athlete in basketball?

A. David Robinson.

Q. The University of Maryland's basketball team was National Invitation Champions in what year?

A. 1972.

Q. Which Oriole pitcher pitched the last ball at Memorial Stadium in 1991?

A. Mike Flanagan.

Q. Who was the Masters Bowling Tournament Champion in 1983?

A. Mike Lastowski of Havre de Grace.

Q. What are the team colors of the Maryland Terps?

A. Red, white, black, and gold.

Q. Which Oriole player hit 46 home runs and drove in 141 runs in 1961.

A. Jim Gentile.

Q. What is the nickname of the Naval Academy's football team?

A. Midshipmen.

Q. Of his many championship bouts during his career, Muhammad Ali had two fights in Landover against what two opponents?

A. Jimmy Young (1976) and Alfredo Evangelista (1977).

Q. Which guns, which could kill a dozen ducks with a single shot, were used by hunters on the Eastern Shore until outlawed in the 1880s?

A. Punts.

Q. Who won the Senior Pistol category at the 1987 National Outdoor Rifle and Pistol Championships?

A. Joseph C. White of Rockville.

Q. The NCAA Division I championship was held for what sport on March 24, 1990 at College Park?

A. Wrestling.

Q. Which popular shortstop, noted for his fancy glove work, joined the Orioles in 1955?

A. Willy Miranda.

Q. Landover is organization headquarters for what NHL team?

A. Washington Capitals.

Q. What affable native of Opelika, Alabama, became Oriole manager in 1962?

A. Billy Hitchcock.

Q. In what town is the Maryland Horse Breeders Association based?

A. Timonium.

Q. How many games did the Orioles lose during their first season?

A. 100.

Q. Picked up by the Baltimore Colts, who was the number one draft choice of the NFL in 1983?

A. John Elway.

Q. Which Baltimore Oriole became the first major leaguer to hit home runs from both sides of the plate in consecutive games?

A. Eddie Murray.

Q. In what year did the Loyola, Maryland, lacrosse team make it to the playoffs for the first time?

A. 1990.

Q. Which sport is popular at Herrington Manor and New Germany state parks?

A. Cross-country skiing.

Q. Which Oriole catcher hit the first home run on opening day in 1954?

A. Clint Courtney.

Q. Where did Maryland lose to Georgia 17-16 in 1973?

A. Peach Bowl.

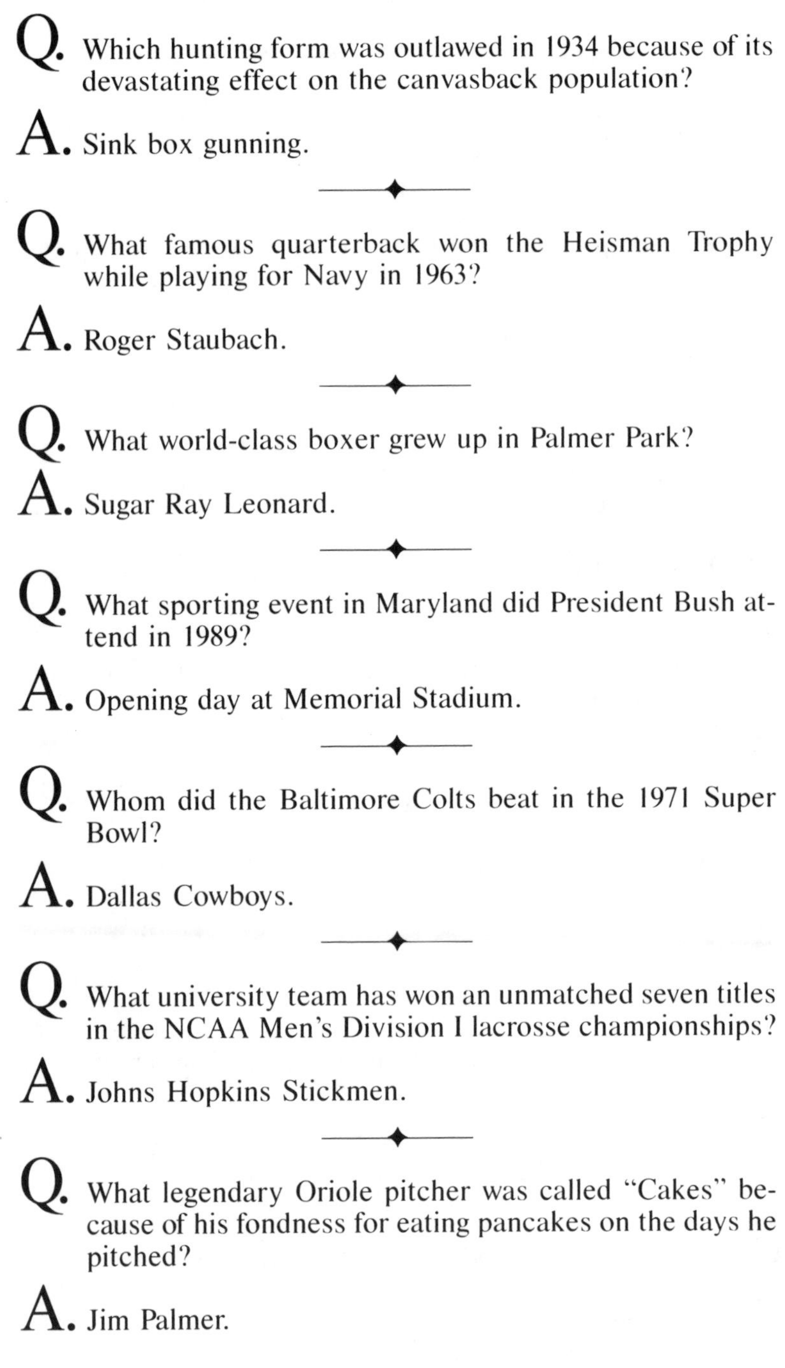

Q. Which hunting form was outlawed in 1934 because of its devastating effect on the canvasback population?

A. Sink box gunning.

⸻✦⸻

Q. What famous quarterback won the Heisman Trophy while playing for Navy in 1963?

A. Roger Staubach.

⸻✦⸻

Q. What world-class boxer grew up in Palmer Park?

A. Sugar Ray Leonard.

⸻✦⸻

Q. What sporting event in Maryland did President Bush attend in 1989?

A. Opening day at Memorial Stadium.

⸻✦⸻

Q. Whom did the Baltimore Colts beat in the 1971 Super Bowl?

A. Dallas Cowboys.

⸻✦⸻

Q. What university team has won an unmatched seven titles in the NCAA Men's Division I lacrosse championships?

A. Johns Hopkins Stickmen.

⸻✦⸻

Q. What legendary Oriole pitcher was called "Cakes" because of his fondness for eating pancakes on the days he pitched?

A. Jim Palmer.

SCIENCE & NATURE

CHAPTER SIX

Q. Rachel Carson, Silver Spring author and zoologist, aroused concern with her 1962 book, *Silent Spring*, because it described what?

A. The potentially dangerous effects of misused insecticides.

◆

Q. What plant is dominant in the fresh tidal river section of the Patuxent marsh?

A. Wild rice.

◆

Q. Birders come at night to Elliott Island to listen to the calls of what secretive birds?

A. Black rails.

◆

Q. What is the largest estuary in the United States?

A. The Chesapeake Bay.

◆

Q. What is the name of the dark-colored river that runs through the vast tidal marshes of Dorchester County?

A. Blackwater.

Q. What industry was found in the George's Creek Valley?

A. Coal mining.

⸻✦⸻

Q. What car was built in Maryland early in the century?

A. The Calvert.

⸻✦⸻

Q. Where are Maple Syrup Days celebrated each winter?

A. Cockeysville, at the Oregon Ridge Nature Center.

⸻✦⸻

Q. What was once considered the most beautiful sailing ship in the United States?

A. *Baltimore Clipper*.

⸻✦⸻

Q. Construction began on July 4, 1828, on which canal project that eventually connected Washington, D.C., and Cumberland, Maryland?

A. Chesapeake and Ohio Canal.

⸻✦⸻

Q. What was the first chartered railroad in the United States?

A. Baltimore and Ohio.

⸻✦⸻

Q. America's first steam locomotive, which operated on the B&O Railroad, had which nickname?

A. Tom Thumb.

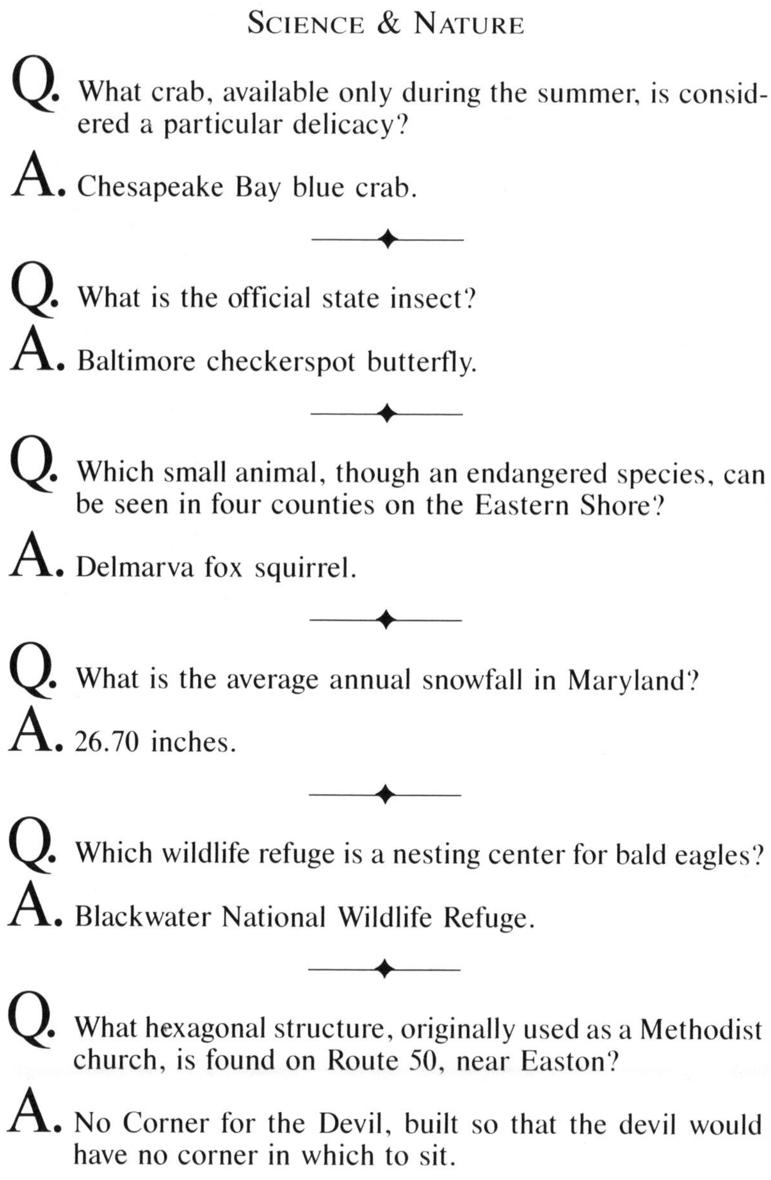

Q. What crab, available only during the summer, is considered a particular delicacy?

A. Chesapeake Bay blue crab.

Q. What is the official state insect?

A. Baltimore checkerspot butterfly.

Q. Which small animal, though an endangered species, can be seen in four counties on the Eastern Shore?

A. Delmarva fox squirrel.

Q. What is the average annual snowfall in Maryland?

A. 26.70 inches.

Q. Which wildlife refuge is a nesting center for bald eagles?

A. Blackwater National Wildlife Refuge.

Q. What hexagonal structure, originally used as a Methodist church, is found on Route 50, near Easton?

A. No Corner for the Devil, built so that the devil would have no corner in which to sit.

Q. Which town is the location of the National Agricultural Library?

A. Beltsville.

Q. Which Baltimore doctor administered the first inoculation against smallpox in 1769?

A. Henry Stevenson.

Q. Which branch of the service has its artillery proving ground in Aberdeen?

A. U.S. Army.

Q. In which park is the Baltimore Zoo located?

A. Druid Hill.

Q. Who invented the first automatic elevator in Baltimore in 1856?

A. James Bates.

Q. What noted bridge opened on July 30, 1952?

A. Chesapeake Bay Bridge.

Q. What is the official state tree?

A. White oak.

Q. The overflow of what river caused the Great Maryland Flood on July 14, 1868?

A. Patapsco.

Q. What hurricane devastated Maryland in 1972?

A. Agnes.

Q. What two cities were connected by the old "Main Branch" on the B&O Railroad?

A. Baltimore and Mount Airy.

Q. Who was the famous Maryland farmer and astronomer who was called the "First Black Man of Science"?

A. Benjamin Banneker.

Q. The U.S. Bureau of the Census is headquartered where?

A. Suitland.

Q. What is the official state flower?

A. Black-eyed Susan.

Q. Where in Baltimore can one sit and be surrounded by sharks?

A. National Aquarium.

Q. Which museum in Wheaton celebrates a once-popular form of transportation?

A. National Capital Trolley Museum.

Q. Who founded the Johns Hopkins Nursing School and was the first superintendent of medical training for the University of Maryland?

A. Louise Parsons.

Q. Which Marylander invented the first electric drill in 1914?

A. Alonzo Decker.

Q. Which Baltimore-born scientist was the first to link cigarette smoking to cancer?

A. Cuyler Hammond.

Q. Who was the noted Johns Hopkins University archaeologist who wrote over 800 books in his field?

A. William Albright.

Q. Which highway in Montgomery County is called the "high technology corridor"?

A. Interstate 270.

Q. Which black Marylander accompanied Admiral Robert Peary on the expedition to the North Pole in 1909?

A. Matthew Henson.

Q. Where was a nuclear power plant built in 1974?

A. Calvert Cliffs.

Q. Where is the Johns Hopkins Applied Physics Laboratory?

A. Columbia.

—✦—

Q. What famous spice company is in Baltimore?

A. McCormick.

—✦—

Q. Acres of waterlilies and goldfish ponds can be seen where?

A. Lilypons Water Gardens, near Buckeystown.

—✦—

Q. In which Prince George's County town is the Goddard Space Flight Center?

A. Greenbelt.

—✦—

Q. Which explorer called Maryland the "Delightsome Land" in 1608?

A. Captain John Smith.

—✦—

Q. Wheaton is the location for what beautiful gardens?

A. Brookside.

—✦—

Q. At what nature preserve in Calvert County can one view the northernmost stand of bald cypress trees in North America?

A. Battle Creek Cypress Swamp Sanctuary.

Q. What kind of travel is celebrated at a museum in Chesapeake Beach?

A. Railway.

Q. What is the name of the naval air base and museum in Lexington Park?

A. Patuxent.

Q. What is the average annual rainfall in Maryland?

A. 41.65 inches.

Q. What is the official state dog?

A. Chesapeake Bay retriever.

Q. Who is Maryland's poultry king?

A. Frank Perdue.

Q. What hydroelectric plant, built in Cecil County in 1928, is one of the largest in the nation?

A. Conowingo Hydroelectric Plant.

Q. In what year did a devasting heat wave in July kill 270 Marylanders?

A. 1972.

Q. Where does Maryland rank among the fifty states in terms of editors per working population?

A. First (in 1980 census data).

Q. According to FBI *Uniform Crime Reports* for 1989, where does Maryland rank in murder rate?

A. Fifth.

Q. Where is the U.S. Army Ordnance Museum?

A. Aberdeen.

Q. What was the first railroad station in the United States?

A. Mount Clare Station in Baltimore, now the B&O Railroad Museum.

Q. What ship is docked at Pier 1 in Baltimore?

A. *U.S. Frigate Constellation.*

Q. Which Baltimore market is the oldest continuously operating market in the United States?

A. Lexington Market, dating from 1782.

Q. What was the main crop in southern Maryland?

A. Tobacco.

Q. Where are the National Institutes of Health based?

A. Bethesda.

Q. What did the legislature designate as the state crustacean in 1989?

A. Maryland blue crab.

Q. Where is the world's oldest operating airport?

A. College Park.

Q. In what center in Laurel does the U.S. Department of the Interior conduct research on endangered species?

A. Patuxent Wildlife Research Center.

Q. What Maryland city has the oldest continuously operating municipal health department in the United States?

A. Baltimore (the Baltimore Department of Health was organized in 1793).

Q. What rare, noisy woodpecker, known by its large white face patch, is native to Maryland and feeds on pines infected with red-heart fungus?

A. Red-cockaded woodpecker.

Q. Where do huge flocks of Canadian geese spend their winters?

A. Blackwater National Wildlife Refuge.

Q. Which town is often called the "Seafood Capital of the World"?

A. Crisfield.

Q. On which island do wild ponies roam free?

A. Assateague Island.

Q. About how many inches of snow fall annually in Garrett County?

A. Eighty.

Q. When did the Main Branch train have its last run?

A. December 31, 1949.

Q. Where is the National Institute of Standards and Technology?

A. Gaithersburg.

Q. What is the official state fish?

A. *Morone Faxatilis* (striped bass or rockfish).

Q. Birders consider which county to be the "Rail Capital of America"?

A. Somerset County.

Q. Where is the National Oceanic and Atmospheric Administration?

A. Rockville.

Q. Where is the Audubon Naturalist Society based?

A. Chevy Chase.

Q. For what is the EconoLodge in Princess Anne noted?

A. It is completely managed by University of Maryland Eastern Shore student hotel interns.

Q. In what arm of the Chesapeake Bay can you find the rare Swainson's warbler?

A. Pocomoke River.

Q. Which town is the location of the National Agricultural Library?

A. Beltsville.

Q. What noted ornithologist and bird artist painted canvasbacks with the Baltimore Harbor in the background?

A. John James Audubon.

Q. Dinah Nuthead became the first woman to be licensed in America in what profession on August 31, 1696?

A. Printing.

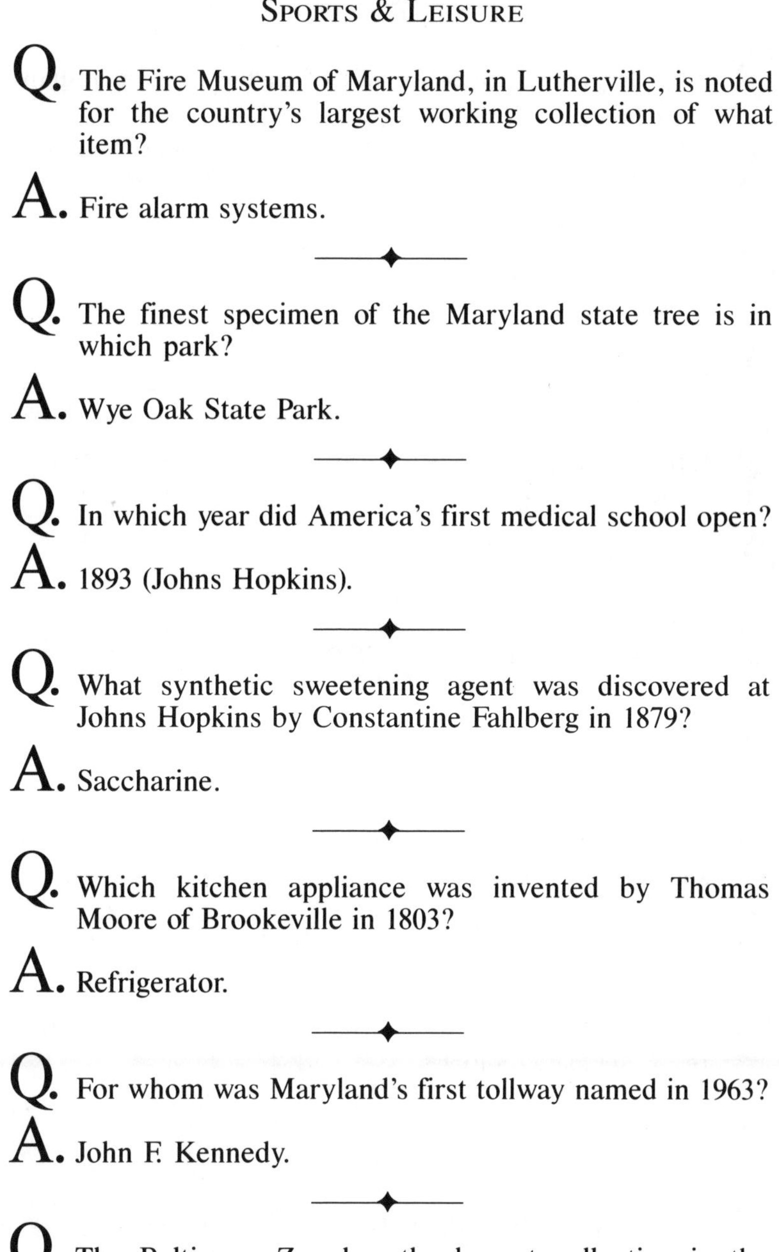

Q. The Fire Museum of Maryland, in Lutherville, is noted for the country's largest working collection of what item?

A. Fire alarm systems.

—◆—

Q. The finest specimen of the Maryland state tree is in which park?

A. Wye Oak State Park.

—◆—

Q. In which year did America's first medical school open?

A. 1893 (Johns Hopkins).

—◆—

Q. What synthetic sweetening agent was discovered at Johns Hopkins by Constantine Fahlberg in 1879?

A. Saccharine.

—◆—

Q. Which kitchen appliance was invented by Thomas Moore of Brookeville in 1803?

A. Refrigerator.

—◆—

Q. For whom was Maryland's first tollway named in 1963?

A. John F. Kennedy.

—◆—

Q. The Baltimore Zoo has the largest collection in the United States of which bird?

A. African black-footed penguins.

Q. What river means "black water" in the original Indian language.

A. Pocomoke.

Q. Which bird is featured on the new Maryland license plate?

A. Great blue heron.

Q. What Baltimore-built ship was the first vessel commissioned by the U.S. Navy?

A. *U.S. Frigate Constellation*.

Q. What boat, used for dredging oysters in the Chesapeake Bay, became Maryland's state boat in 1985?

A. Skipjack.

Q. The shell of what creature was designated the State fossil shell in 1984?

A. An extinct snail, *Ecphora quadricostata*.

Q. The world's first telegraph line was erected in 1844 between what two cities?

A. Baltimore and Washington.

Q. To what does the slogan "Born in Baltimore—raised everywhere" refer?

A. The umbrella, which was first manufactured in Baltimore in 1828.

Q. Which town hosts a Waterfowl Festival in November?

A. Easton.

———✦———

Q. Where is the Chesapeake Bay Maritime Museum?

A. St. Michael's.

———✦———

Q. The Ward Foundation's Wildfowl Art Museum at Salisbury State College is noted for what collection?

A. Decorative bird carvings, including many antique decoys.

———✦———

Q. What is the name of the famous ponies on Assateague Island?

A. Chincoteague.

———✦———

Q. Dredging and tonging are methods for harvesting what seafood?

A. Oysters.

———✦———

Q. What western Maryland hunter is remembered by a flintlock rifle, on display at the Smithsonian Museum?

A. Meshach Browning.

———✦———

Q. What was decided by the Jenkins-Black Award of 1877?

A. The boundary between Maryland and Virginia for oyster fishing.

Q. What does *airish* mean in Eastern Shore dialect?

A. Cold and windy.

Q. What is the local shorebird of the Chincoteague salt marshes?

A. Willet.

Q. What were the three types of sailing vessels used in harvesting oysters?

A. Pungies, bugeyes, and skipjacks.

Q. The first elevated electric railway in the United States was built in 1893 in what city?

A. Baltimore.

Q. For how many miles does the Appalachian Trail run in Maryland?

A. Thirty-eight.

Q. Where can you visit a museum of life-saving artifacts?

A. The Ocean City Life Saving Station Museum.

Q. Where is the Brannock Maritime Museum?

A. Cambridge.

Q. What kind of museum in Hebron will delight children?

A. The Chesapeake Fire Museum.

Q. Where does Maryland rank nationally in number of scientists and engineers per population?

A. Sixth (1990 census).

Q. The skeleton of what kind of ship was recovered from Watts Creek in 1969?

A. Pungy.

Q. What is the male crab called on the Eastern Shore?

A. Jimmy.

Q. What unusual garden is found on the Jacksonville Pike fourteen miles north of Towson?

A. Ladew Topiary Gardens.

Q. What do Eastern Shore men call small clams?

A. Little nicks.

Q. To the watermen, what is a big catch of oysters called?

A. Jag.

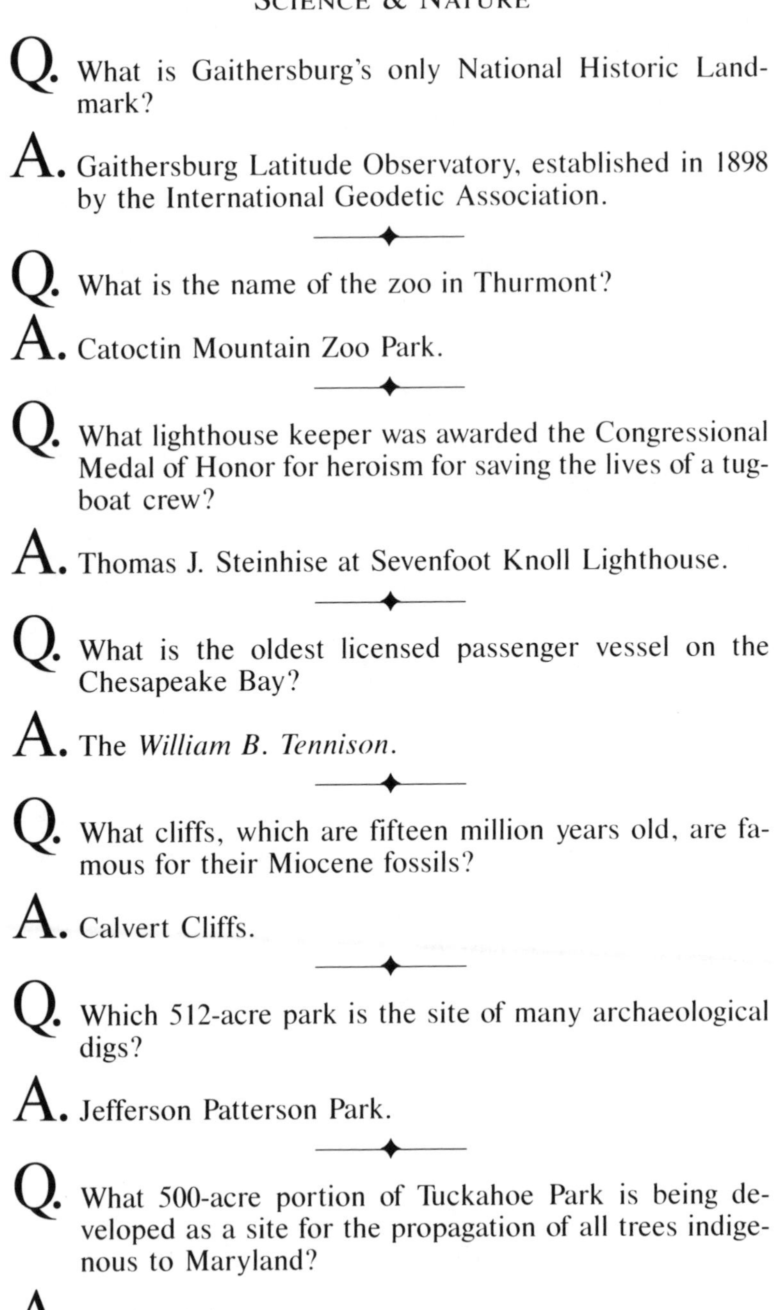

Q. What is Gaithersburg's only National Historic Landmark?

A. Gaithersburg Latitude Observatory, established in 1898 by the International Geodetic Association.

Q. What is the name of the zoo in Thurmont?

A. Catoctin Mountain Zoo Park.

Q. What lighthouse keeper was awarded the Congressional Medal of Honor for heroism for saving the lives of a tugboat crew?

A. Thomas J. Steinhise at Sevenfoot Knoll Lighthouse.

Q. What is the oldest licensed passenger vessel on the Chesapeake Bay?

A. The *William B. Tennison*.

Q. What cliffs, which are fifteen million years old, are famous for their Miocene fossils?

A. Calvert Cliffs.

Q. Which 512-acre park is the site of many archaeological digs?

A. Jefferson Patterson Park.

Q. What 500-acre portion of Tuckahoe Park is being developed as a site for the propagation of all trees indigenous to Maryland?

A. Adkins Arboretum.

Q. What dinosaur once lived exclusively in Maryland?

A. Priconodon, whose fossils can be found along Route 1 near Beltsville and Laurel.

—✦—

Q. What screwpile lighthouse, now resting in Baltimore's Inner Harbor, was the last all-iron lighthouse on the Bay?

A. Sevenfoot Knoll Lighthouse.

—✦—

Q. What is the more common name for Baltimore's Patterson Park Observatory?

A. Pagoda.

—✦—

Q. Which fungus entered Maryland around 1910 and destroyed some of its most important trees?

A. Chestnut blight.

—✦—

Q. Where is the Nature Conservancy headquartered?

A. Chevy Chase.

—✦—

Q. Where is the National Weather Association?

A. Temple Hills.

—✦—

Q. Under which tree, legend says, did the early settlers and the Choptank Indians confer?

A. Treaty Oak in Dorchester County.

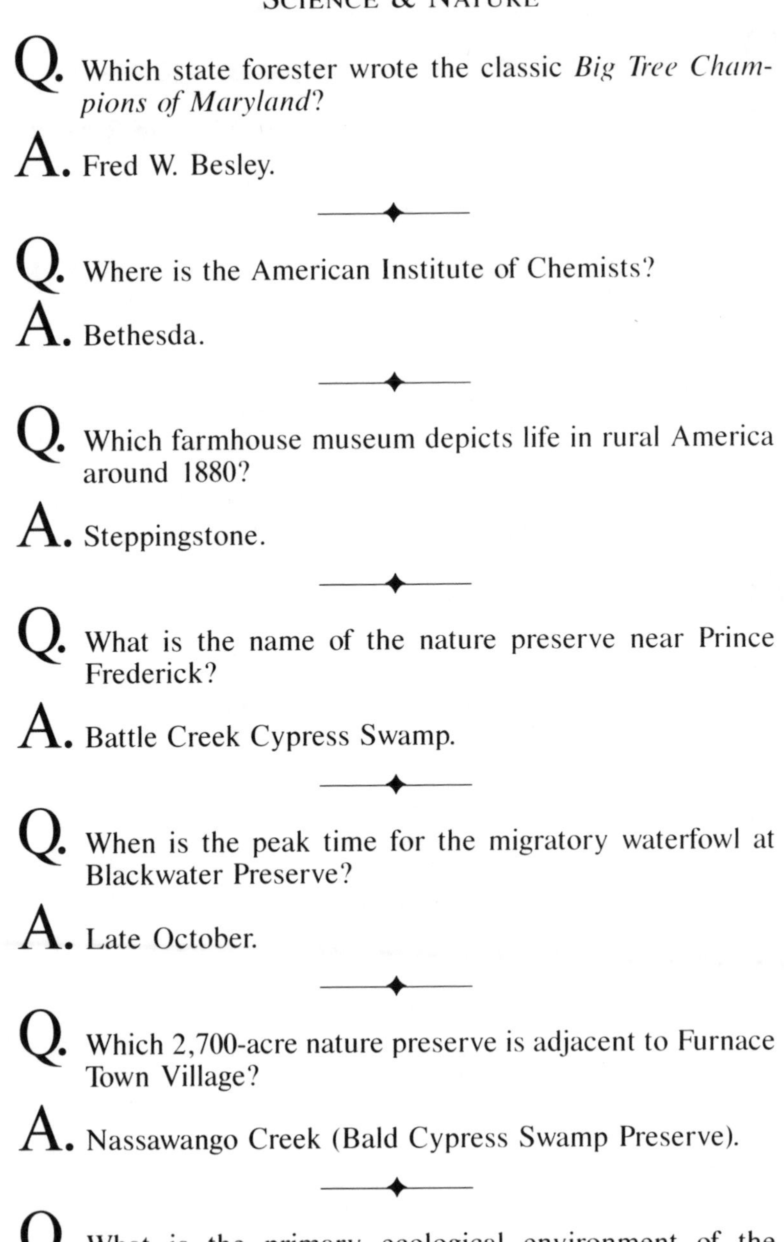

Q. Which state forester wrote the classic *Big Tree Champions of Maryland*?

A. Fred W. Besley.

Q. Where is the American Institute of Chemists?

A. Bethesda.

Q. Which farmhouse museum depicts life in rural America around 1880?

A. Steppingstone.

Q. What is the name of the nature preserve near Prince Frederick?

A. Battle Creek Cypress Swamp.

Q. When is the peak time for the migratory waterfowl at Blackwater Preserve?

A. Late October.

Q. Which 2,700-acre nature preserve is adjacent to Furnace Town Village?

A. Nassawango Creek (Bald Cypress Swamp Preserve).

Q. What is the primary ecological environment of the Blackwater Preserve?

A. Tidal marsh.

Q. When did the Maryland Forestry Association inaugurate the Big Tree Contest?

A. 1925.

Q. Which three endangered bird species are seen occasionally in the Blackwater Refuge?

A. Bald eagle, peregrine falcon, and least tern.

Q. When do the ospreys begin to leave the Blackwater Refuge?

A. September.

Q. What crustacean performs a phenomenal spawning ritual in the Chesapeake Bay each May and June?

A. Horseshoe crab.

Q. Which creature scurries across the sand on lower Chesapeake Bay beaches and then disappears into a hole?

A. Ghost crab or sand crab.

Q. Which precious metal was once mined along the C&O Canal near Potomac?

A. Gold.

Q. What kind of small deer can be seen on Assateague Island?

A. Japanese sika deer.

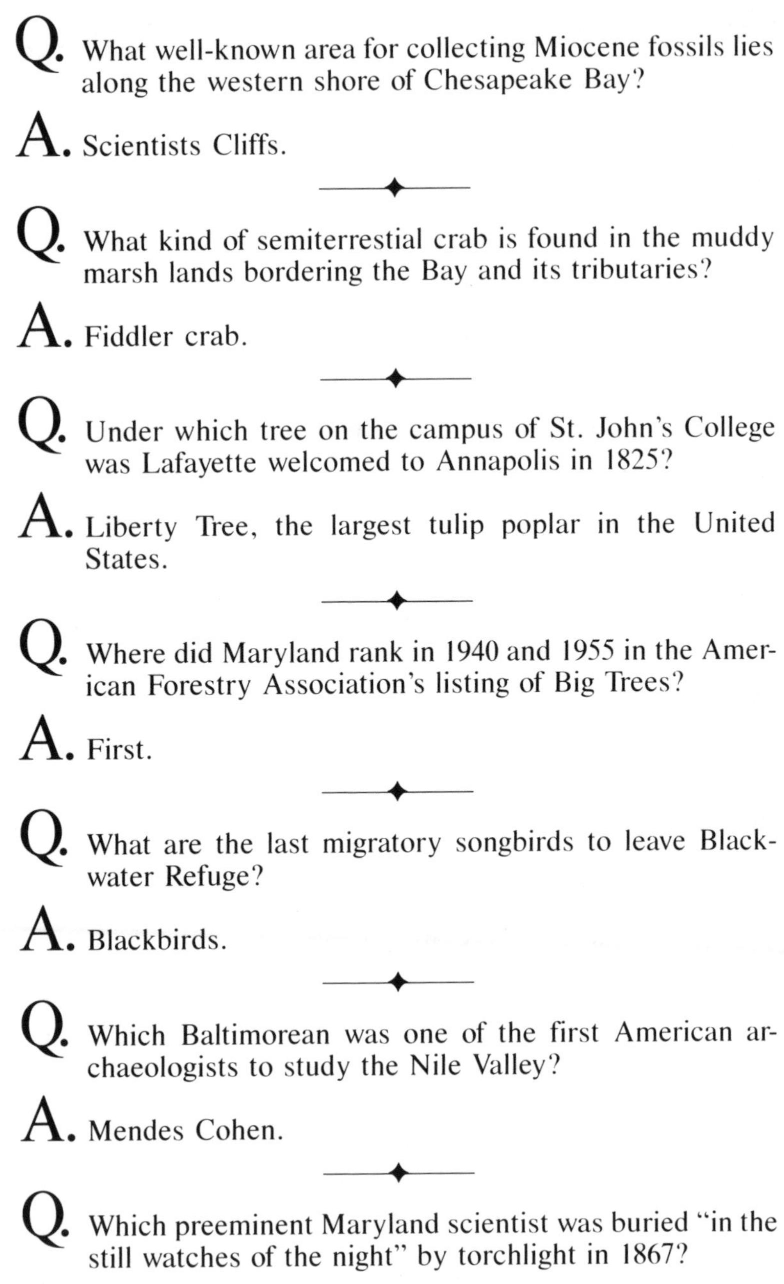

Q. What well-known area for collecting Miocene fossils lies along the western shore of Chesapeake Bay?

A. Scientists Cliffs.

Q. What kind of semiterrestial crab is found in the muddy marsh lands bordering the Bay and its tributaries?

A. Fiddler crab.

Q. Under which tree on the campus of St. John's College was Lafayette welcomed to Annapolis in 1825?

A. Liberty Tree, the largest tulip poplar in the United States.

Q. Where did Maryland rank in 1940 and 1955 in the American Forestry Association's listing of Big Trees?

A. First.

Q. What are the last migratory songbirds to leave Blackwater Refuge?

A. Blackbirds.

Q. Which Baltimorean was one of the first American archaeologists to study the Nile Valley?

A. Mendes Cohen.

Q. Which preeminent Maryland scientist was buried "in the still watches of the night" by torchlight in 1867?

A. John Henry Alexander.

Q. What kind of swan arrives in early November at the Blackwater Refuge?

A. Tundra swan.

Q. Where was the first crematorium in Maryland?

A. Loudon Park Cemetery (1889).

Q. Which museum in Cambridge has a collection of old fishing tools, Indian artifacts, and archaeological findings?

A. Neild.

Q. What nineteenth-cetury method of transportation can still be found in Wicomico County?

A. Flatboat ferries, two of which still cross the Wicomico River daily.

Q. When did a tidal wave cause Assateague Island to become separated from the mainland?

A. 1933.

Q. Which Caroline County state park is rich in native American lore?

A. Martinak.

Q. Where does Maryland rank in number of active physicians per population?

A. Second to Massachusetts (1990 census).

Q. What do the dwarf ponies on Assateague Island eat?

A. Seaweed and shore grasses.

Q. Where is the largest overcup oak tree in the United States?

A. Tuckahoe State Park.

Q. What is a female crab called on the Eastern Shore?

A. Sook or sooky.

Q. Where is the largest still-standing covered bridge in Maryland?

A. Gilpin's Falls near North East.

Q. What island refuge in Kent County serves as a major feeding and resting place for wintering waterfowl?

A. Eastern Neck National Wildlife Refuge.

Q. What is said to be the oldest "free running" (no cable) ferry in the United States?

A. Tred Avon Ferry in Oxford.

Q. Which town was once a shipbuilding center, noted for its slick Baltimore clippers?

A. Oxford.

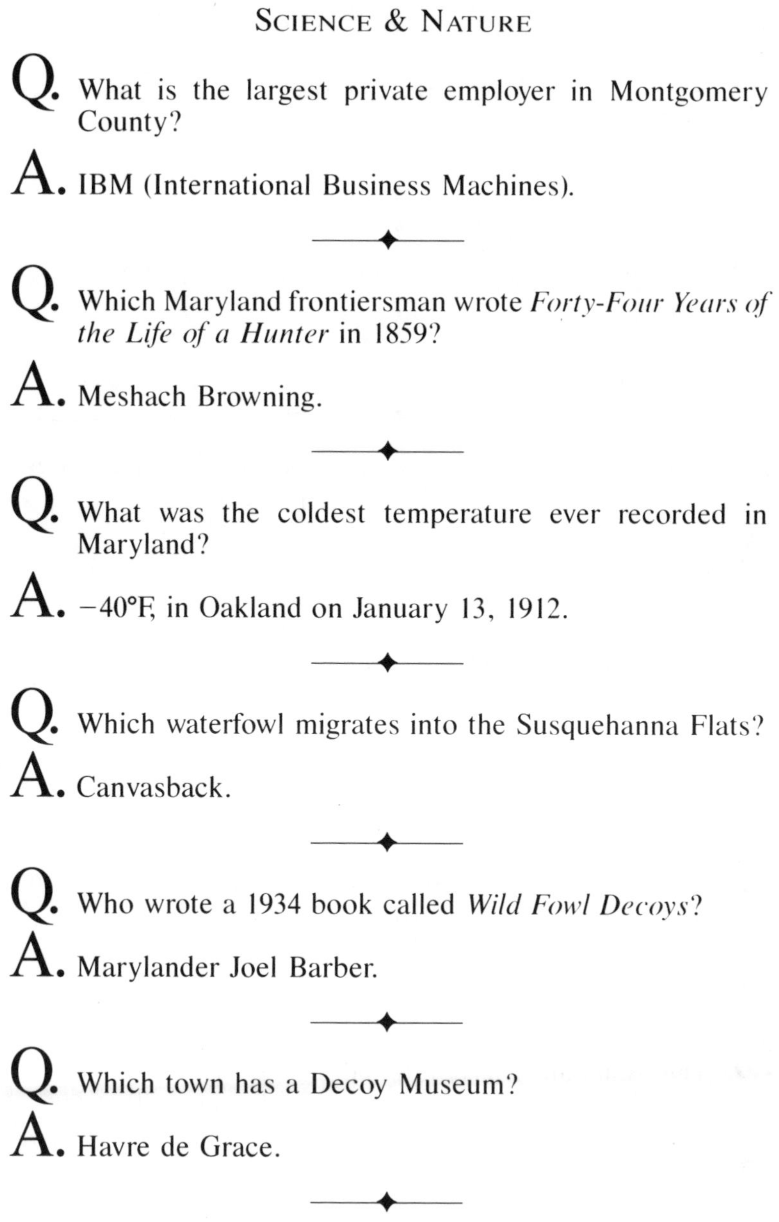

Q. What is the largest private employer in Montgomery County?

A. IBM (International Business Machines).

Q. Which Maryland frontiersman wrote *Forty-Four Years of the Life of a Hunter* in 1859?

A. Meshach Browning.

Q. What was the coldest temperature ever recorded in Maryland?

A. −40°F, in Oakland on January 13, 1912.

Q. Which waterfowl migrates into the Susquehanna Flats?

A. Canvasback.

Q. Who wrote a 1934 book called *Wild Fowl Decoys*?

A. Marylander Joel Barber.

Q. Which town has a Decoy Museum?

A. Havre de Grace.

Q. Which Baltimorean invented a mechanical reaper one year before Cyrus McCormick?

A. Obed Hussey.

Q. What is the primary attraction of the Susquehanna Flats for migrating waterfowl?

A. Abundant beds of celery grass.

Q. What "floating sculptures" are both a form of folk art and a boon to hunters?

A. Decoys.

Q. Who invented the Baltimore heater, a nineteenth-century precursor to the modern furnace?

A. John Latrobe.

Q. What extraordinary invention is credited to Christian Eisenbrandt of Baltimore?

A. A coffin with a spring lock within, to prevent people from being buried alive.

Q. Which Silver Spring scientist wrote a classic book entitled *The Sea Around Us*?

A. Rachel Carson.

Q. The Bollman Truss Railroad Bridge in Savage is the world's last surviving example of what kind of bridge?

A. Semisuspension.

Q. Which Baltimore hospital established the first intensive care unit in the nation in 1952?

A. Johns Hopkins.

Q. What park near Hagerstown has a forty-two-acre man-made lake?

A. Greenbrier State Park.

Q. What does the Hagerstown Roundhouse Museum preserve and promote?

A. Locomotives.

Q. Which Bethesda-based writer is author of *The Pleasures of Watching Birds*?

A. Lola Oberman.

Q. What color flag must be flown to indicate that a boatman is down, diving for oysters?

A. Red flag with a white slash.

Q. What is the name of the farmers' cooperative headquartered in southern Prince George's County?

A. Maryland Tobacco Growers Association.

Q. Which owner of a Maryland mansion, called Medical Hall, received the first medical degree awarded in America?

A. Dr. John Archer.

Q. What is the name for the boat used by crabbers to tow their gear through the water?

A. Scraping boat.

Albert and Shirley Menendez are residents of Gaithersburg, Maryland. Albert is the author of a number of books including *Christmas in the White House*. Shirley is a former librarian and is active in the field of education.